The Psychology of Money

Unveiling the Secrets of Financial Behavior

WORKBOOK

DR. MAXWELL SHIMBA

Published in Manhattan, New York by Shimba Publishing, LLC.

Shimba Publishing LLC

Table of Contents

The Psychology of Money Workbook

INTRODUCTION WORKSHEET

The Interplay of Mind and Money

Learning Objectives

☐ Recognize money as a psychological and emotional construct, not merely a financial tool
☐ Identify how personal history and beliefs shape financial behavior
☐ Establish personal intentions for this workbook journey
☐ Commit to self-reflection rather than quick fixes

Reflection Questions

Take 10-15 minutes with these questions. Write without editing or judging your answers.

When you hear the word "money," what emotions arise immediately?
(Circle all that apply)

Anxiety / Hope / Shame / Freedom / Guilt / Power / Fear / Excitement / Insecurity / Pride / Numbness / Obligation / Other: __________

Unpack one circled emotion below:

This emotion most often shows up when:

____

I believe this emotion comes from:

____

Do you associate money more with freedom, stress, power, or security? Why?

My primary association: ☐ Freedom ☐ Stress ☐ Power ☐ Security ☐ Mixed/Other

Because:

____

What is one financial behavior you want to understand—not just change?

Behavior:

____

What I currently do:

____

What I wish I did:

____

What I'm curious to learn about *why* I do this:

____

____

Personal Intention Statement

Complete this sentence with honesty, not idealism.

By completing this workbook, I intend to change my relationship with money by:

____

____

____

My Commitment Level (circle one):

I am here to observe | I am ready to understand | I am ready to make changes | I am skeptical but willing

Signature: ________________________ **Date:** ______________

CHAPTER 01

The Foundations of Financial Psychology

1.1 THE MONEY MINDSET

Beliefs That Shape Behavior

Key Concepts Review

Term	Definition	In My Own Words
Money Mindset	The invisible internal architecture of beliefs, assumptions, and automatic thoughts governing financial decisions	
Scarcity Mindset	Zero-sum thinking; belief that resources are fixed; hyper-vigilance; short-term orientation	
Abundance Mindset	Belief that value can be created; long-term vision; agency; security from capability, not just cash	
Financial Scripts	Deeply held, often unconscious beliefs about money formed in childhood	
Neuroplasticity	The brain's ability to rewire itself through repeated thoughts and behaviors	

Exercise 1.1.1: Your Earliest Money Memories

Write freely. Do not edit. These are archaeological data points.

My earliest memory of money is (age, place, what happened):

Growing up, money in my home felt mostly like:

☐ A source of safety and calm
☐ A source of conflict and stress
☐ Something scarce we never had enough of
☐ Something abundant but not discussed
☐ A secret—we didn't talk about it
☐ A tool for rewards and punishments
☐ A burden to manage
☐ Other: ____

What did adults argue or agree about regarding money?

Arguments about:

____

Agreements about:

____

What was *not* said but implied?

____

____

Exercise 1.1.2: Family Money Scripts Inventory

Complete these sentences with your first, unfiltered response.

"Money doesn't grow on..."

____

"Rich people are..."

____

"People like us..."

____

"We can't afford..."

____

"You have to work hard for..."

____

"Money is the root of..."

____

"Save for a rainy day because..."

____

"I feel guilty when I spend money on..."

____

"I feel proud when I spend money on..."

____

"I deserve..."

____

Circle the scripts above that still influence you today.

Trace one script to its origin:

This script came from: ☐ Parent ☐ Grandparent ☐ Culture ☐ Early experience

The message was delivered by: ☐ Words ☐ Silence ☐ Emotional atmosphere ☐ Actions

This script has cost me:

____

Exercise 1.1.3: Scarcity vs. Abundance Diagnostic

Rate each statement honestly from 1 (Strongly Disagree) to 5 (Strongly Agree).

Statement	1	2	3	4	5
I worry about money even when things are financially stable.	☐	☐	☐	☐	☐

Statement	1	2	3	4	5
I believe opportunities for income and growth can always be created.	☐	☐	☐	☐	☐
I avoid looking at my bank accounts or bills.	☐	☐	☐	☐	☐
I trust my ability to recover from financial setbacks.	☐	☐	☐	☐	☐
I feel anxious when I spend money on myself.	☐	☐	☐	☐	☐
I believe the economic "pie" is fixed—if others gain, I lose.	☐	☐	☐	☐	☐
I can name three financial goals I'm working toward.	☐	☐	☐	☐	☐
Market downturns feel like personal threats.	☐	☐	☐	☐	☐
I am able to delay gratification for long-term gain.	☐	☐	☐	☐	☐
I believe my financial situation will improve over time.	☐	☐	☐	☐	☐

Scoring:

Scarcity Indicators: Items 1, 3, 5, 6, 8 (reverse score for 5, 3, 1 = high scarcity)

Abundance Indicators: Items 2, 4, 7, 9, 10 (add scores)

My tendency leans toward: ☐ Strong Scarcity ☐ Moderate Scarcity ☐ Mixed ☐ Moderate Abundance ☐ Strong Abundance

Reflection:

Where did I learn my scarcity patterns?

____

Where did I learn my abundance patterns?

____

One area where my scarcity mindset actually *protects* me:

____

One area where my scarcity mindset *limits* me:

____

Exercise 1.1.4: Money and Identity

Complete these sentences. The goal is self-awareness, not self-judgment.

When I have money, I feel: ____

When I lack money, I feel: ______________________________

Money makes me feel valuable when: ______________________________

If I lost all my money tomorrow, I would still be: ______________________________

Identity Check

Which statement best describes your dominant relationship with money?

☐ **Money is a tool.** It serves my goals. I try to use it efficiently and detach emotionally.

☐ **Money is a scorecard.** It measures my success, competence, and worth relative to others.

☐ **Money is security.** Its primary purpose is to protect me from uncertainty and threat.

☐ **Money is freedom.** It buys me options, time, and the ability to say no.

☐ **Money is status.** It signals my position, taste, and belonging.

☐ **Money is evil/corrupting.** I'm uncomfortable with it and distrust those who have it.

☐ **Money is care.** It's how I express love, provide for family, and show generosity.

☐ **Mixed/Other:** ____________________________________

How does this dominant identity serve you? ____________________________________

How does this dominant identity limit you? ____________________________________

Exercise 1.1.5: The Neuroscience Pause – Applied Practice

Next time you experience financial stress, use this protocol immediately after (or ideally during).

Date: __________ **Situation:** ____________________________

What I felt in my body: ____________________________________

The thought that triggered the feeling: ____________________________________

I was afraid of losing: ☐ Money ☐ Security ☐ Status ☐ Control ☐ Love/Approval ☐ Identity ☐ Other: _____

Is this a real, current threat or an emotional memory from the past?

☐ Real threat (concrete, verifiable, actionable)
☐ Emotional memory (feels threatening but is not actually

dangerous)
☐ Mixed/Unsure

Evidence that this is a memory/script, not current reality: ___________________________

What would my future self (5 years older/wiser) advise me to do right now?

____

What would I advise a dear friend in this exact situation? ___________________________

____

One small action I can take from a place of agency, not fear: ___________________________

____

Exercise 1.1.6: Behavioral Experiment – 7-Day Financial Mindfulness

Choose ONE experiment for the next 7 days. Commit. Observe. Do not judge.

☐ **Experiment A: The Emotion Tracker**
Each time you spend money or check your finances, pause and write:

Day	Transaction/Event	Emotion Before	Emotion After	Urge (What I wanted to do)	Actual Action
1					
2					
3					
4					
5					
6					
7					

☐ Experiment B: The Daily Glance

Each day, open your primary banking app. Look at your balance for 10 seconds. Do nothing else. Close the app. Note your emotional reaction.

☐ Experiment C: The Intentional Micro-Save

Each day, transfer $1 (or $5) to a savings account. As you do it, say aloud or silently: "*I am capable of building security.*"

☐ Experiment D: The 48-Hour Pause

When you want to make an impulse purchase (any non-essential over $20), wait 48 hours. Journal the urge. After 48 hours, decide.

7-Day Experiment Reflection (Complete on Day 8)

Experiment I chose: ☐ A ☐ B ☐ C ☐ D

What I noticed about my automatic financial patterns:

____

____

The strongest emotion I encountered was:

____

What surprised me:

____

What was harder than expected:

____

What was easier than expected:

____

One thing I learned about myself:

____

I will continue: ☐ This experiment ☐ A modified version ☐ A new experiment next week

Exercise 1.1.7: Reframing – Installing New Code

For each limiting belief, write a new, evidence-based alternative.

Old Script (from my family/culture)	Evidence This Isn't Always True	New Empowering Belief
Example: "Money doesn't grow on trees"	I have generated income multiple ways. Resources can be cultivated.	"I am capable of generating value and earning income through my skills."

Exercise 1.1.8: Environmental and Social Engineering Audit

My Financial Information Diet:

Media I consume that reinforces financial anxiety/comparison:

____

Media I could consume that educates/inspires healthy finance:

____

One account I will unfollow/mute this week:

____

One account I will follow/subscribe to:

____

My Financial Tribe:

People in my life whose financial relationship I admire (for their peace, not their net worth):

1. ______________________________
2. ______________________________

One conversation I will initiate this month about values-based money: ______________________________

Ritual Design:

One new financial task I will pair with pleasure:

"*I will [financial task] while enjoying [pleasurable activity].*"

Example: "I will review my net worth while drinking my favorite coffee on Saturday morning."

1.2 COGNITIVE BIASES IN FINANCIAL DECISION-MAKING

Key Concepts Review

Bias	Definition	Example
Loss Aversion	Pain of loss is ~2x stronger than pleasure of gain	
Anchoring	Over-relying on first piece of information	
Availability Heuristic	Judging likelihood by how easily examples come to mind	
Confirmation Bias	Seeking/remembering info that confirms existing beliefs	
Overconfidence	Overestimating knowledge, skill, or predictive accuracy	

Bias	Definition	Example
Disposition Effect	Selling winners too early, holding losers too long	
Endowment Effect	Valuing something more simply because you own it	
Mental Accounting	Treating money differently based on arbitrary categories	
Sunk Cost Fallacy	Continuing due to past investment, ignoring future value	
Present Bias	Overvaluing immediate rewards at expense of future	
Outcome Bias	Judging decision quality by outcome, not process	

Exercise 1.2.1: Bias Self-Audit

For each bias, check if you've experienced it and describe one example.

Bias	☐ Experienced	Example from My Financial Life
Loss Aversion	☐	
Anchoring	☐	
Availability Heuristic	☐	
Confirmation Bias	☐	
Overconfidence	☐	
Disposition Effect	☐	
Endowment Effect	☐	
Mental Accounting	☐	
Sunk Cost Fallacy	☐	
Present Bias	☐	
Outcome Bias	☐	

Exercise 1.2.2: Loss Aversion Inventory

A loss feels ____ times more powerful than a gain to me. (Circle)
1x 1.5x 2x 2.5x 3x+

Describe a time you held onto a losing investment/asset too long because you "didn't want to realize the loss":

Describe a time you sold a winning investment/asset too early because you wanted to "lock in gains":

How has loss aversion affected your willingness to:

Take necessary risks:

Change financial institutions/products:

Negotiate salary/prices:

Exercise 1.2.3: Confirmation Bias – Breaking the Echo Chamber

Identify a current financial belief you hold strongly (e.g., "Real estate is the best investment," "I'm bad at investing," "The market is about to crash"):

____

Where did I learn this belief? ____

What sources do I regularly consume that reinforce this belief? ____

Who/what would disagree with this belief? ____

Assignment: Go find the *strongest, most intelligent argument against* your belief. Summarize it here:

____

____

After reading the counterargument, my belief is:

☐ Unchanged ☐ Slightly modified ☐ Significantly modified ☐ I'm now uncertain

What did this exercise teach me about my own thinking? ____

____

Exercise 1.2.4: Overconfidence Calibration

Without looking anything up, answer these three questions with a 90% confidence range (a range you are 90% certain contains the true answer).

1. **What was the S&P 500's annual return in 2022?**
   My 90% confidence range: ____% to ____%
   Actual answer: -19.44%
2. **What is the current US federal funds interest rate?**
   My 90% confidence range: ____% to ____%
   Actual answer: _______%
3. **What percentage of US household income goes to taxes on average?**
   My 90% confidence range: ____% to ____%
   Actual answer: ~27%

How many of your 90% ranges actually contained the correct answer? ___ out of 3

Reflection: What does this reveal about my tendency toward over precision? ____

Exercise 1.2.5: Mental Accounting – Mapping Your Internal Accounts

List the mental "buckets" you unconsciously use for money.

Mental Account Label	Source of Money (e.g., paycheck, gift, bonus)	How I Feel About Spending This	Rules for This Account
Example: "Fun Money"	Side hustle, birthday gifts	Free, guilt-free	Can spend on anything under $50

1.

2.

3.

4.

5.

Reality Check: Money is fungible. A dollar is a dollar regardless of source.

One way I will merge my mental accounts toward more rational allocation: ______________________________

Exercise 1.2.6: Sunk Cost Autopsy

Describe a situation where you threw good money after bad:

What I invested initially (time/money/effort):

____

Why I continued:

____

What I was afraid of admitting:

____

What it ultimately cost me:

____

What I learned:

____

____

Exercise 1.2.7: Present Bias – The Future Self Interview

Close your eyes. Imagine yourself 20 years older. Now answer these questions as that future self.

Dear Younger Me,

The one thing I wish you had started sooner was:

____

____

The purchases you made that you barely remember now:

____

The money you saved/invested that made the biggest difference: ______________________________________

You worried about ________, but looking back, it wasn't as catastrophic as you feared.

Your future is better because you decided to:

____

With love,

Your [Age ______] Self

Exercise 1.2.8: Building Anti-Bias Systems

Design your personal bias countermeasures.

My Investment Policy Statement (IPS) – Draft

My primary financial goal(s):

____

My time horizon: ☐ <5 years ☐ 5-10 years ☐ 10-20 years ☐ 20+ years

My target asset allocation (stocks/bonds/cash): ____% / ____% / ____%

I will rebalance my portfolio: ☐ Quarterly ☐ Annually ☐ When allocation drifts > ___%

My "If-Then" Rules (Implementation Intentions):

Trigger/Cue	My Pre-Committed Response
IF the market drops >15%	THEN I will ____________
IF I feel FOMO about a hot investment	THEN I will ____________
IF I want to make an impulse purchase >$100	THEN I will ____________
IF I receive a bonus or windfall	THEN I will ____________
IF I am tempted to check my portfolio daily	THEN I will ____________

My Decision Journal Protocol:

Before any major financial decision (>$500 or any investment), I will write:

1. Decision I am making: ______________________________
2. My reasoning (including my confidence level 0-100%): ______________
3. What would have to be true for this to be a mistake? ______________
4. Date: __________ Signature: ________________________

I will review this entry in 6-12 months.

1.3 EMOTIONAL UNDERPINNINGS OF MONETARY CHOICES

Key Concepts Review

Emotion	Evolutionary Function	Financial Distortion	Wise Integration
Fear	Protection from threat	Panic selling, paralysis, hoarding	Signal to do due diligence
Greed	Resource acquisition	Speculative bubbles, excessive leverage	Channel into creation/growth
Hope	Motivation toward goals	Irrational exuberance, magical thinking	Discipline + optimism
Regret	Learning from mistakes	Myopic loss aversion, inaction	Process over outcome
Shame	Social cohesion/signaling	Secrecy, avoidance, self-sabotage	Separate behavior from identity

Exercise 1.3.1: Your Financial Emotional Profile

For each emotion, rate how often it influences your financial decisions:

Emotion	Rarely (1)	Sometimes (2)	Often (3)	Frequently (4)	Dominant (5)
Fear	☐	☐	☐	☐	☐
Greed	☐	☐	☐	☐	☐
Hope	☐	☐	☐	☐	☐
Regret	☐	☐	☐	☐	☐
Shame	☐	☐	☐	☐	☐
Guilt	☐	☐	☐	☐	☐
Joy	☐	☐	☐	☐	☐
Envy	☐	☐	☐	☐	☐
Pride	☐	☐	☐	☐	☐

My top three financial emotions: 1. ________ 2. ________ 3. ________

What triggers each? ____

What am I usually seeking or avoiding when I act on these emotions? ______________________________

____

____

Exercise 1.3.2: The Somatic Marker Inventory – Listening to Your Body

Your body knows before your mind does. Map your financial body signals.

Financial Situation	Physical Sensation	Location in Body	What It's Telling Me
Example: Checking 401(k) after a drop	Tightness, shallow breath	Chest, stomach	"This feels like danger. Pause before acting."
Receiving a windfall			
Paying a large bill			

Financial Situation	Physical Sensation	Location in Body	What It's Telling Me
Considering a risky investment			
Looking at credit card debt			
Making a charitable gift			
Buying something for myself			

Exercise 1.3.3: Fear Deconstruction Protocol

Next time fear arises around a financial decision, work this protocol.

What specific outcome am I afraid of? ____

On a scale of 1-10, how likely is this outcome? ____ (1 = almost impossible, 10 = certain)

If this outcome happened, what would be the actual consequences? ______________________________

____

Could I survive it? ☐ Yes ☐ With difficulty ☐ Unsure

What resources (financial, social, psychological) would help me cope? ______________________________

____

What is within my control right now? ______________________________

One small action I can take to reduce risk OR increase resilience: ______________________________

____

Exercise 1.3.4: Greed/FOMO Diagnostic

Think of a time you chased a "hot" investment, bought something you couldn't afford, or felt desperate not to miss out.

What was the story I told myself? ______________________________

____

What did I believe this purchase/investment would give me? ___________________________

(☐ Status ☐ Validation ☐ Excitement ☐ Security ☐ Belonging ☐ Freedom)

Did it deliver that? ☐ Yes ☐ Partially ☐ No

What was the real cost? ___________________________

What deeper need was I trying to meet? ___________________________

How else could I meet that need without financial risk? ___________________________

Exercise 1.3.5: Regret Re-framing

Regret ("I should have...")	Reframe ("Given what I knew then, I...")	What I Learned
I should have bought that stock	Given what I knew then, I chose safety.	I prefer avoiding loss over chasing gain.

Exercise 1.3.6: Shame – Naming It to Tame It

What financial fact about myself would I be most embarrassed for others to know?

Who taught me that this is shameful? ____

If I told one trusted, non-judgmental person, what might happen? ____

Separating behavior from identity:

I am not ______________________________ (e.g., "a financially irresponsible person")

I am someone who made a choice to ____

I can choose differently next time by: ____

Exercise 1.3.7: Emotional Regulation Strategy Design

Choose 2-3 strategies to install as automatic responses.

☐ **Antecedent-Focused (Prevent the emotion)**

- I will check my portfolio: ☐ Weekly ☐ Monthly ☐ Quarterly (not daily)
- I will delete these apps: ______________________________
- I will unfollow these triggers: ______________________________
- I will automate: ☐ Savings ☐ Bill pay ☐ Investments

☐ **Cognitive Reappraisal (Change the meaning)**

- Instead of "I'm losing money," I will say: "______________________________"
- Instead of "I missed out," I will say: "______________________________"
- Instead of "I can't afford this," I will say: "______________________________"
- My "And" statement for financial fear: "I feel _____ AND ______________________________"

☐ **Response-Focused (Manage the moment)**

- My 10-breath rule: When I feel financial panic, I will ______________________________
- My 24-hour rule: For any purchase over $_____, I will wait 24 hours.
- My physical reset: When stressed, I will: ☐ Walk ☐ Breathe ☐ Stretch ☐ Other: ____________________

☐ **Positive Emotion Cultivation**

- My weekly financial gratitude: Three things about my finances I'm grateful for:

1. ______
2. ______
3. ______

- How I will celebrate financial process, not just outcomes: ______
- One small act of financial generosity I will practice this month: ______

1.4 THE ROLE OF EARLY LIFE AND CULTURAL IMPRINTING

Key Concepts Review

Concept	Definition	My Application
Financial Socialization	Process of absorbing financial norms, values, behaviors from environment	
Money Scripts (Klontz)	Unconscious core beliefs about money	

Concept	Definition	My Application
	(Avoidance, Worship, Status, Vigilance)	
Individualism vs. Collectivism	Self-reliance vs. group/family financial interdependence	
Uncertainty Avoidance	Preference for clear rules and stability vs. comfort with ambiguity	
Long-Term Orientation	Future rewards vs. present/short-term focus	

Exercise 1.4.1: The Family Money Genogram

Draw or describe your family's financial lineage across three generations.

Generation	Key Financial Events	Money Scripts	Emotional Climate	What Was Passed Down

Grandparents

Parents

Me

What patterns do I see repeating? ____

____

What pattern do I want to continue? ____

What pattern do I want to break? ____

____

Exercise 1.4.2: The Klontz Money Script Assessment

Rate how much you agree with each statement (1 = Strongly Disagree, 5 = Strongly Agree).

Money Avoidance:

- Money is the root of all evil. 1 2 3 4 5
- Rich people are greedy/corrupt. 1 2 3 4 5
- I don't deserve a lot of money. 1 2 3 4 5

Money Worship:

- More money will solve my problems. 1 2 3 4 5
- I'll never have enough money. 1 2 3 4 5
- If I had more money, everything would be better. 1 2 3 4 5

Money Status:

- My net worth equals my self-worth. 1 2 3 4 5
- People judge me by my financial success. 1 2 3 4 5
- I need to display my success. 1 2 3 4 5

Money Vigilance:

- Money should be saved, not spent. 1 2 3 4 5
- It's not safe to talk about money. 1 2 3 4 5
- I worry about money constantly. 1 2 3 4 5

My dominant money script(s): ______________________________

This script came from: ______________________________

This script has served me by: ______________________________

This script has cost me: ______________________________

One way I will update this script: ______________________________

____

Exercise 1.4.3: Cultural Financial Profile

Using Hofstede's dimensions, reflect on your cultural financial programming.

Individualism vs. Collectivism:

My culture emphasizes: ☐ Personal achievement & self-reliance ☐ Group/family interdependence

This shows up in my finances as:

____

One collectivist value I want to keep:

____

One individualist value I want to adopt:

____

____

Uncertainty Avoidance:

My culture's attitude toward financial risk: ☐ Avoid at all costs ☐ Calculated risk is acceptable

This shows up as:

____

One way this protects me:

One way this limits me:

Long-Term vs. Short-Term Orientation:

My culture emphasizes: ☐ Future rewards, thrift, perseverance ☐ Present enjoyment, quick results

This shows up as:

I want to strengthen my: ☐ Long-term patience ☐ Present-moment enjoyment

Indulgence vs. Restraint:

My culture's attitude toward spending on enjoyment: ☐ "Work hard, play hard" ☐ Saving is virtue, spending is guilt

This shows up as:

A healthy balance for me would be:

Exercise 1.4.4: The Immigrant/Intergenerational Imprint (if applicable)

My family's immigration/economic history includes: ______________________________

____

The financial legacy of this experience is: ______________________________

____

This has gifted me: ______________________________

This has burdened me: ______________________________

What I want my financial legacy to be for the next generation: ______________________________

____

____

Exercise 1.4.5: Deconstruction & Differentiation

List your core financial beliefs. Then ask: "Is this mine, or did I inherit it?"

Financial Belief	Origin (Family/Culture/Personal Experience)	Is This Serving Me?	I Choose To: (Keep/Modify/Release)
Example: "Debt is always shameful."	Parents struggled with debt, never recovered.	No—it prevents strategic use of credit.	Modify: "Debt for consumption is risky; debt for appreciating assets can be strategic."

Exercise 1.4.6: Code-Switching Practice

A situation where my inherited financial script conflicts with my current context:

The old script says: ______________________________

The current context requires: ______________________________

How I can honor the wisdom of the old script while adapting to the new context:

____

____

1.5 CASE STUDY: SCARCITY VS. ABUNDANCE

A Twenty-Year Journey – Michael and David

____

Exercise 1.5.1: Reader Identification

Which investor do you most identify with at this stage of your life?

☐ Michael (Scarcity: protective, fearful, reactive)
☐ David (Abundance: engaged, process-driven, resilient)
☐ A mix of both (describe):

____

Why? ______________________________

Exercise 1.5.2: Critical Analysis

What advantages did David have that weren't just "mindset"? ______________________________

What disadvantages did Michael face that weren't just "mindset"? ______________________________

What systemic factors (family background, education, access) influence scarcity vs. abundance mindsets?

Exercise 1.5.3: Applying the Framework to Your Own Financial Timeline

Map your own "Michael and David" moments.

Year/Period	Event	My Response (Scarcity or Abundance?)	What I Was Feeling	What I Would Do Differently Now

Exercise 1.5.4: The Path for Michael – Your Personal Rewiring Plan

If you identified with Michael, complete this section.

1. Financial Therapy/Exploration:

The childhood origins of my scarcity terror:

One financial trauma I need to separate from present reality:

2. System Over Willpower:

One financial decision I will automate this week:

____

One investment I will set up to be "Do Not Touch":

____

One person I will give permission to help me stay the course:

____

3. Start Small & Build Evidence:

My tiny, safe investment experiment:

I will invest $_______ in a broad index fund on _______ (date).

I will commit to not selling for at least _______ months.

I will observe my emotional response without acting.

Post-Experiment Reflection:

What I felt:

____

What I learned:

____

____

Exercise 1.5.5: Your Financial Psychology Growth Plan

Three months from now, I will know my mindset is shifting when I:

1. ____

2.
3.

One sentence to remember from this chapter:

CHAPTER 1 ACTION PLAN

One belief I will challenge this month:

One behavior I will practice consistently:

One system I will put in place:

One truth to remember:

"What has been learned can be unlearned. What has been wired can be rewired."

Chapter 1 Completion Checklist

☐ I have completed all reflection exercises
☐ I have identified at least one core money script
☐ I have named my dominant financial emotion(s)
☐ I have designed at least one anti-bias rule
☐ I have completed one behavioral experiment
☐ I have drafted my intention for this workbook journey
☐ I am ready to proceed to Chapter 2

Date Completed: ____________________________________

My Key Insight from Chapter 1:

CHAPTER 02

Emotion, Fear, and Financial Decision-Making

The Investor's Psyche

Learning Objectives

☐ Identify personal emotional triggers behind financial choices
☐ Distinguish fear-based decisions from wisdom-based decisions
☐ Understand the neurobiology of financial fear and greed
☐ Practice emotional regulation strategies for money moments
☐ Build an inner "circuit breaker" between impulse and action

---

Key Concepts Review

Term	Definition	In My Own Words
System 1 (Fast Brain)	Automatic, emotional, intuitive thinking; operates with little effort	
System 2 (Slow Brain)	Deliberate, logical, analytical thinking; requires effort and attention	
Amygdala Hijack	When the brain's fear center overrides the prefrontal cortex during financial stress	
Loss Aversion	The pain of losing is psychologically ~2x more powerful than the pleasure of gaining	
Anterior Insula	Brain region associated with physical pain and disgust; activates during financial loss	

Term	Definition	In My Own Words
Nucleus Accumbens	Brain's reward center; floods with dopamine during anticipated or realized gains	
Disposition Effect	Selling winners too early, holding losers too long (driven by loss aversion)	
FOMO	Fear Of Missing Out; anxiety-driven urge to participate in perceived opportunities	
Cognitive Reappraisal	Changing the emotional impact of a situation by changing its meaning	
Implementation Intention	"If-Then" planning that pre-commits to a behavior in response to a specific cue	

EXERCISE 2.1: EMOTIONAL MONEY TRIGGERS

Mapping Your Financial Emotional Landscape

Part A: Trigger Identification

List 5-7 situations where money triggers a strong emotional reaction in you.

Situation	**Primary Emotion(s) Felt**	**Intensity (1-10)**	**Typical Action/Urge**
Example: Checking 401(k) after market drop	**Fear, Dread**	**8**	**Urge to sell everything**
1.			
2.			
3.			
4.			

Situation	Primary Emotion(s) Felt	Intensity (1-10)	Typical Action/Urge
5.			
6.			
7.			

Part B: Emotion Frequency Audit

Over the past 30 days, how often have you experienced these emotions related to money?

Emotion	Never	1-2 times	3-5 times	6-10 times	10+ times
Fear/Anxiety	☐	☐	☐	☐	☐
Greed/"More" Urge	☐	☐	☐	☐	☐

Emotion	Never	1-2 times	3-5 times	6-10 times	10+ times
Regret	☐	☐	☐	☐	☐
Shame	☐	☐	☐	☐	☐
Guilt	☐	☐	☐	☐	☐
Excitement/Anticipation	☐	☐	☐	☐	☐
Envy/Comparison	☐	☐	☐	☐	☐
Relief	☐	☐	☐	☐	☐
Pride	☐	☐	☐	☐	☐

My three most frequent financial emotions:

1. ________________ 2. ________________ 3. ________________

What pattern do I notice? ________________________________

____

____

Part C: Emotional Signature Discovery

For your strongest financial emotion, complete this deep dive.

Emotion: ______________________________

What typically triggers this emotion? ______________________________

Where do I feel it in my body? ______________________________

What thought runs through my mind? ______________________________

What story do I tell myself about this situation? ______________________________

What is the deeper need beneath this emotion?
(☐ Security ☐ Control ☐ Validation ☐ Belonging ☐ Freedom ☐ Love ☐ Other: ____)

What is this emotion trying to protect me from? ______________________________

What is this emotion trying to move me toward? ______________________________

EXERCISE 2.2: THE FEAR AUDIT

Confronting Your Financial Fears

Part A: The Fear Hierarchy

Rank your financial fears from most to least threatening.

Rank	Fear	On a scale of 1-10, how likely is this?	On a scale of 1-10, how devastating would this be?
1			
2			
3			
4			
5			

Part B: Fear Genealogy

What financial outcome do I fear the most?

Where did this fear originate?
☐ Childhood experience ☐ Parent's fear ☐ Past financial loss ☐ Media/news ☐ Cultural narrative ☐ Other: ___________________

Describe the originating event or message: ____

Is this fear:
☐ Rational (based on current, verifiable threat)
☐ Historical (based on past event that is no longer present)
☐ Imagined (based on a scenario that has not happened)
☐ A mix (explain):
____

Evidence that this fear is NOT currently true: ____

Part C: The "What If" Ladder – Facing the Worst Case

Take your top fear and walk it down to the ground.

I am afraid that: ___

If that happened, then: ___

And if that happened, then: ___

And if that happened, then: ___

And if that happened, then: ___

And if that happened, the worst part would be: ___

Could I survive that? ☐ Yes ☐ With help ☐ I'm not sure

What resources (financial, social, psychological) would I have even in that worst case?

1. ___
2. ___
3. ___

What have I survived before that gives me confidence? ___

Part D: Fear's Cost-Benefit Analysis

What Has This Fear Cost Me?	What Has This Fear Protected Me From?
Example: Missed investment gains	Example: Avoiding panic-selling during volatility

Does this fear still serve me, or has it become a liability? ____________________

EXERCISE 2.3: THE NEUROBIOLOGY OF FEAR AND GREED

Your Brain on Money

Part A: Amygdala Hijack – Personal Case Study

Describe a time you made a financial decision from pure panic or fear.

Date/Context: ______________________________

What was the trigger? ______________________________

What did you feel in your body? ______________________________

What impulse did you have? ______________________________

What did you actually do? ______________________________

What was the outcome? ______________________________

Looking back, what would your calmer, wiser self have advised? ______________________________

Part B: Dopamine Loop – The Thrill of the Chase

Describe a time you were driven by FOMO, greed, or the thrill of a potential gain.

Date/Context: ________________________________

What was the "story" you told yourself? ________________________________

What did the anticipation feel like? ________________________________

What did you do? ________________________________

What was the outcome? ________________________________

Was it as satisfying as you expected? ☐ Yes ☐ No ☐ Briefly

What did this experience teach you about your own "reward system"? ________________________________

Part C: The 2.5x Rule – Your Personal Loss Aversion Coefficient

Imagine this scenario:

You have two options:

- **Option A:** A guaranteed gain of $500
- **Option B:** A 50% chance to gain $1,000 and a 50% chance to gain $0

Which do you choose? ☐ A (sure $500) ☐ B (gamble for $1,000)

Now imagine:

- **Option C:** A guaranteed loss of $500
- **Option D:** A 50% chance to lose $1,000 and a 50% chance to lose $0

Which do you choose? ☐ C (sure -$500) ☐ D (gamble to avoid loss)

Interpretation:

Most people choose **A** (risk-averse in gains) and **D** (risk-seeking in losses). This is loss aversion.

How much more painful is a loss than a gain for you? (Circle)

1x | 1.5x | 2x | 2.5x | 3x | 4x | 5x+

Example in my life of this asymmetry: ______________________________

____

____

EXERCISE 2.4: EMOTIONAL SPENDING VS. SAVING

The Hidden Drivers of Cash Flow

Part A: Emotional Spending Inventory

Review your last 5-10 discretionary purchases. What emotion drove each?

Purchase	Amount	Emotion Before	Emotion After	Need I Was Trying to Meet
Example: New jacket	$180	Bored, inadequate	Brief excitement, then guilt	Validation, "fresh start"
1.				
2.				
3.				
4.				
5.				

Patterns I notice: ______________________________

One emotion I frequently "spend on": ____________________

A non-spending way to meet that need: ____________________

5.

Part B: Emotional Saving/Avoidance Inventory

Review your last 5-10 times you AVOIDED financial tasks. What emotion drove each?

Avoided Task	Amount	Emotion Before	Justification	Actual Consequence
Example: Opening 401(k) statement	Unknown	Fear, shame	"I'll check later"	Missed rebalancing opportunity

1.

2.

3.

4.

5.

Patterns I notice: ______________________________

One emotion that causes me to freeze financially: ______________________________

One small step I can take to face this fear this week: ______________________________

EXERCISE 2.5: THE FEAR-BASED DECISION PROTOCOL

Your Pre-Commitment Circuit Breaker

Part A: My Red Flags – Early Warning Signs

List your personal signals that you are in an emotional, reactive state.

Physical signals (e.g., clenched jaw, shallow breath, racing heart):

1. ______________________________
2. ______________________________
3. ______________________________

Mental signals (e.g., racing thoughts, catastrophizing, black-and-white thinking):

1. ____________________
2. ____________________
3. ____________________

Behavioral signals (e.g., checking accounts obsessively, avoiding bills):

1. ____________________
2. ____________________
3. ____________________

____

Part B: My Pause Protocol

When I notice these red flags, I will do this BEFORE making any financial decision:

Step 1: Physical Reset (Choose one)

☐ Take 10 slow, deep breaths (inhale 4, hold 4, exhale 6)
☐ Stand up and walk for 5 minutes
☐ Drink a glass of water slowly
☐ Splash cold water on my face
☐ Other:

____

Step 2: Mental Shift (Choose one)

☐ Ask: "Is this a real threat or an old memory?"
☐ Ask: "What would I advise my best friend in this situation?"
☐ Ask: "Will this matter in 1 year? 5 years?"
☐ Read my Investment Policy Statement or financial mission

statement
☐ Other:

____

Step 3: Time Delay (Choose one)

☐ 24-hour rule: I will wait 24 hours before any action
☐ 72-hour rule: I will wait 72 hours before any action
☐ 7-day rule: I will wait 7 days before any action

My complete Pause Protocol (written as a script):

"When I feel [RED FLAG SIGNAL], I will immediately [PHYSICAL RESET]. Then I will ask myself [MENTAL SHIFT QUESTION]. Finally, I will wait [TIME DELAY] before taking any action."

____

____

____

Part C: My "If-Then" Implementation Intentions

Complete each statement with your pre-committed response.

If This Happens...	Then I Will...
IF the stock market drops more than 10% in a month...	THEN I will ______________________

If This Happens...	Then I Will...
IF I feel a strong urge to buy something I haven't budgeted for...	THEN I will ______________________
IF I receive an unexpected windfall (bonus, gift, inheritance)...	THEN I will ______________________
IF I see a "hot investment tip" on social media...	THEN I will ______________________
IF I feel tempted to check my portfolio for the third time today...	THEN I will ______________________
IF I feel shame about a past financial mistake...	THEN I will ______________________

EXERCISE 2.6: COGNITIVE REAPPRAISAL – REFRAMING FINANCIAL FEAR

Changing the Story

Part A: Reframe Practice

For each fear-based thought, practice writing an alternative, evidence-based reframe.

Automatic Fear Thought	Reappraisal (New Frame)
"I'm losing money!"	"My investments are experiencing expected volatility. I own the same companies; the price is temporarily lower."
"I missed out on huge gains!"	
"The market is crashing!"	

Automatic Fear Thought	Reappraisal (New Frame)
"I'll never have enough for retirement."	
"I'm so stupid for that purchase."	
"Everyone else is getting rich but me."	
"I can't afford this."	

Part B: Personal Reframe Cards

Create 3 personal reframes for your most common financial fears.

Fear Trigger: ____

Old Thought: ____

New Thought: ____

Fear Trigger: ____

Old Thought: ____

New Thought: ____

Fear Trigger: ____

Old Thought: ____

New Thought: ____

Part C: The "And" Technique

Instead of trying to eliminate fear, hold both the fear AND the rational plan.

"I feel [FEAR] AND I have [RESOURCE/PLAN]."

Examples:

- *"I feel afraid about this market drop AND I have a 20-year investment horizon."*
- *"I feel regret about that purchase AND I am learning to be more mindful."*

My "And" Statements:

1. I feel ________________ AND I have ____________________
2. I feel ________________ AND I am ______________________
3. I feel ________________ AND I know ___________________

EXERCISE 2.7: THE DECISION JOURNAL – PROCESS OVER OUTCOME

Learning from Your Financial Choices

Part A: Major Decision Pre-Mortem

Before a significant financial decision, complete this form.

Date: ____________ **Decision:** _________________________________

My current emotional state (circle all that apply):
Calm / Excited / Anxious / Fearful / Confident / Confused / Pressured

My reasoning for this decision: ____

What I expect will happen: ____________________________________

What could go wrong? ____________________________________

What would have to be true for this to be a mistake? __________________

My confidence level in this decision (0-100%): ____%

If I'm wrong, how will I know? ______________________________

Signature: ___________________________

Part B: Decision Post-Mortem (6-12 months later)

Date: ______________________________

Original Decision: ______________________________

Actual outcome: ______________________________

Was the outcome:
☐ Better than expected ☐ As expected ☐ Worse than expected

Was the decision process sound, given what I knew at the time?
☐ Yes ☐ Partially ☐ No

What did I learn from this outcome? ______________________________

____

Would I make the same decision again with the same information?
☐ Yes ☐ No ☐ I would modify it by:

____

____

EXERCISE 2.8: EMOTIONAL REGULATION STRATEGIES – YOUR PERSONAL TOOLKIT

Part A: Strategy Selection

Choose 3-5 strategies you will actively practice.

☐ STRATEGY 1: REDUCE EXPOSURE TO TRIGGERS (Antecedent-Focused)

- I will check my investment accounts: ☐ Weekly ☐ Monthly ☐ Quarterly (not daily)
- I will delete these apps from my phone: ____
- I will unsubscribe from these financial news sources: ____
- I will unfollow/mute these social media accounts: ____

☐ STRATEGY 2: AUTOMATE DECISIONS (Pre-Commitment)

- I will automate my monthly savings transfer of $_______
- I will automate my investment contribution of $_______
- I will automate bill payments for: ____
- I will enroll in my employer's auto-escalation retirement feature: ☐ Yes

☐ STRATEGY 3: COGNITIVE REAPPRAISAL (Change the Meaning)

- I will practice reframing market downturns as "sales," not "losses"
- I will practice reframing budgeting as "freedom allocation," not "deprivation"
- I will keep my reframe cards on my phone/in my wallet
- My weekly reappraisal practice:

  ____

☐ STRATEGY 4: PHYSIOLOGICAL REGULATION (Calm the Body)

- My breathing reset: ☐ 4-7-8 technique ☐ Box breathing ☐ 10 slow exhales
- My movement reset: ☐ 5-minute walk ☐ Stretch break ☐ Other: ________
- I will practice this daily (not just in crisis): ☐ Yes ☐ I commit to trying

☐ STRATEGY 5: THE PAUSE-AND-PROTOCOL RULE

- My cooling-off period for non-essential purchases over $_____ is: _____ hours
- My cooling-off period for selling investments is: _____ hours/days
- I will write a one-page rationale before any major portfolio change: ☐ Yes

☐ STRATEGY 6: CULTIVATE POSITIVE FINANCIAL EMOTIONS

- My weekly financial gratitude practice:

  ____
- How I will celebrate financial PROCESS (not just outcomes): ______________________________________

- One small act of financial generosity I will practice this month: ___________________________________

Part B: My Emotional Regulation Commitment

The strategy I will practice THIS WEEK: ___________________________________

When I will practice it: ___________________________________

How I will track my progress: ___________________________________

Who I will tell about my commitment (accountability partner): ___________________________________

EXERCISE 2.9: THE 2008 FINANCIAL CRISIS – A PSYCHOLOGICAL AUTOPSY

Learning from Collective Fear

Part A: Personal Memory (If you were investing in 2008-2009)

What do you remember feeling during the crisis? ______________________________

What did you do? ______________________________

What do you wish you had done differently? ______________________________

Part B: If You Weren't Investing Yet

What stories have you heard or absorbed about 2008? ______________

How has that event shaped your financial fears or beliefs? ____

What would the "successful minority" have done differently? (Review pages 98-101)

1.
2.
3.

Part C: Lessons Applied

What is the "2008" of your generation? (A market/economic event that triggered mass fear)

How did you respond? ____

What would your "Investment Policy Statement" have told you to do? ____

What one rule will you put in place NOW for the NEXT crisis? ____

BEHAVIORAL PRACTICE: 7-DAY EMOTIONAL AWARENESS EXPERIMENT

Experiment Choice: ☐ 24-Hour Rule Practice ☐ Emotion Tracking ☐ Reframe Practice ☐ Pause Protocol

My goal for this week: ____

Daily Log

Day	Financial Event/Decision	Emotion Before	Pause Used? (Y/N)	Emotion After	What I Learned
1					
2					
3					
4					
5					
6					
7					

End-of-Week Reflection

What was the most common emotional trigger this week? ____

What strategy was most helpful? ______________________________

What was harder than expected? ______________________________

What was easier than expected? ______________________________

One thing I learned about my emotional patterns: ______________________________

I will continue: ☐ This experiment ☐ A modified version ☐ A new experiment next week

FAITH INTEGRATION

Spirit and Finance

Scripture Reflection

"For God has not given us a spirit of fear, but of power, love, and a sound mind." (2 Timothy 1:7)

What fear about money has been dominating my thoughts? ______________________________

What would it look like to approach this financial situation with:

POWER (agency, capability, action)?

____

LOVE (connection, generosity, perspective)?

____

A SOUND MIND (clarity, wisdom, self-control)?

Prayer / Intention for This Chapter

Write a brief prayer, intention, or affirmation for your financial emotions.

CHAPTER 2 ACTION PLAN

One fear I will face this month:

One emotional trigger I will prepare for:

One regulation strategy I will install as a habit:

One truth to remember:

"The goal is not emotional elimination, but emotional literacy—the ability to recognize, name, understand, and ultimately harness these powerful forces."

CHAPTER 2 COMPLETION CHECKLIST

☐ I have completed all reflection exercises
☐ I have identified my top financial fear and its origin
☐ I have named my most frequent financial emotions
☐ I have created my personal Pause Protocol
☐ I have written 2-3 "If-Then" implementation intentions
☐ I have practiced at least one cognitive reframe
☐ I have completed the 7-day behavioral experiment
☐ I am ready to proceed to Chapter 3

Date Completed: ______________________________

My Key Insight from Chapter 2:

"You are both the sailor and the shipwright. Your emotions are the sea—sometimes calm, often turbulent. Your system—your IPS, your automation, your mindfulness—is the hull, the sails, and the navigation equipment. You cannot control the sea, but you can build a vessel so seaworthy that you can sail through any storm."

CHAPTER 03

Risk, Uncertainty, and Faith

Navigating the Unknown with Wisdom

Learning Objectives

☐ Understand your personal psychological responses to financial uncertainty
☐ Distinguish between risk (measurable) and uncertainty (unmeasurable)
☐ Develop a faith-informed framework for assessing financial risks
☐ Learn to separate productive risk-taking from reckless speculation
☐ Build a decision-making process that integrates information, wisdom, and discernment

Key Concepts Review

Term	Definition	In My Own Words
Risk	Uncertainty that can be measured, quantified, and assigned probabilities	
Uncertainty	Unknown unknowns; situations where probabilities cannot be calculated	
Loss Aversion	The tendency to prefer avoiding losses over acquiring equivalent gains	
Regret Aversion	Fear of making a decision that will later cause painful regret	

Term	Definition	In My Own Words
Probability Neglect	Tendency to ignore statistical probabilities when emotionally engaged	
Normalcy Bias	Underestimating the possibility of disruption; believing things will continue as they are	
Faith-Based Risk	Taking calculated action not despite uncertainty, but grounded in values and trust	
Prudence (Phronesis)	Practical wisdom; knowing the right action in a specific context	
Margin of Safety	Building buffers to withstand worst-case scenarios	

EXERCISE 3.1: RISK PROFILE ASSESSMENT

Understanding Your Risk DNA

Part A: Self-Assessment Inventory

Rate each statement honestly from 1 (Strongly Disagree) to 5 (Strongly Agree).

Statement	1	2	3	4	5
I am comfortable making decisions without complete information.	☐	☐	☐	☐	☐
I prefer knowing exactly what will happen with my money.	☐	☐	☐	☐	☐
I am willing to invest in things that could lose value for the chance of growth.	☐	☐	☐	☐	☐
The possibility of losing money keeps me up at night.	☐	☐	☐	☐	☐

Statement	1	2	3	4	5
I have avoided opportunities because I was afraid of failure.	☐	☐	☐	☐	☐
I believe taking calculated risks is necessary for growth.	☐	☐	☐	☐	☐
I worry more about what I might lose than what I might gain.	☐	☐	☐	☐	☐
I can bounce back quickly from financial setbacks.	☐	☐	☐	☐	☐
I often compare my financial decisions to what others are doing.	☐	☐	☐	☐	☐
I trust my ability to handle unexpected financial challenges.	☐	☐	☐	☐	☐

Part B: Scoring & Interpretation

Risk Tolerance Score: Add scores for items 1, 3, 8, 10. Subtract scores for items 2, 4, 5, 6 (reverse), 7, 9.

Simplified: Higher scores on 1,3,8,10 + lower scores on 2,4,5,7,9 = higher risk tolerance*

My overall tendency leans toward:

☐ **Risk-Averse** – I prefer certainty and preservation. Loss feels very painful. I need high confidence to act.

☐ **Risk-Neutral** – I can take calculated risks but need clear analysis. I balance fear and opportunity.

☐ **Risk-Tolerant** – I'm comfortable with uncertainty. I see potential gains more than potential losses.

☐ **Risk-Seeking** – I am drawn to high-risk, high-reward situations. Excitement is part of the decision.

Part C: Reflection

How accurate does this assessment feel? ______________________________

Where did my risk profile come from?
☐ Childhood/family modeling ☐ Past financial success ☐ Past financial trauma ☐ Personality/temperament ☐ Cultural background ☐ Other: ___________

How has my risk profile served me? _________________________________

How has my risk profile limited me? ___________________________________

One area where I wish I took MORE risk: ______________________________

One area where I wish I took LESS risk: _______________________________

EXERCISE 3.2: RISK VS. UNCERTAINTY – LEARNING TO DISTINGUISH

Knowing What You Don't Know

Part A: Categorization Practice

For each situation, mark whether it is primarily RISK (measurable) or UNCERTAINTY (unmeasurable).

Situation	Risk (Measurable)	Uncertainty (Unmeasurable)
The historical probability of the S&P	☐	☐

Situation	Risk (Measurable)	Uncertainty (Unmeasurable)
500 declining 10% in a given year		
Whether AI will make your profession obsolete in 15 years	☐	☐
The chance of needing a major car repair in the next 12 months	☐	☐
What tax rates will be when you retire	☐	☐
The probability of losing your job in your current industry	☐	☐
Whether your adult child will make wise	☐	☐

Situation	Risk (Measurable)	Uncertainty (Unmeasurable)
financial decisions with their inheritance		
The odds of a house fire in your zip code	☐	☐
What a cryptocurrency will be worth in 5 years	☐	☐

What pattern do you notice? ______________________________

Why does this distinction matter? ______________________________

Part B: My Personal Risk/Uncertainty Map

Take a current financial concern and analyze it.

Current financial decision/situation I am wrestling with: ____

What aspects of this are RISK (can be researched, modeled, assigned probabilities)?

1. ____________________
2. ____________________
3. ____________________

What aspects of this are UNCERTAINTY (cannot be known, must be tolerated)?

1. ____________________
2. ____________________
3. ____________________

Where am I spending energy trying to turn uncertainty into risk? ____________________

____

What would change if I accepted this uncertainty as a permanent condition, not a problem to solve?

____

____

EXERCISE 3.3: PAST RISK REVIEW

Learning from Your Risk-Taking History

Part A: Risk Retrospective

Identify three financial risks you have taken in your life—one that worked out well, one that didn't, and one you avoided.

Risk #1 – THE SUCCESS

Describe the risk: ______________________________

What information did I have at the time? ______________________________

What was my emotional state? ______________________________

What was the outcome? ______________________________

What did this experience teach me about myself? ______________________________

What did this experience teach me about risk? ______________________________

Risk #2 – THE FAILURE OR MISTAKE

Describe the risk: ______________________________

What information did I have at the time? ______________________________

What was my emotional state? ______________________________

What was the outcome? ______________________________

Was the decision process sound, given what I knew then? ☐ Yes ☐ No ☐ Partially

What did this experience teach me? ______________________________

What would I do differently now? ____

Risk #3 – THE MISSED OPPORTUNITY (Risk I Avoided)

Describe the opportunity I did NOT take: ____

Why did I avoid it? ____

What was I afraid of? ____

Looking back, was this avoidance justified or limiting? ____

What would I do differently now? ____

Part B: Pattern Identification

What patterns do I see across my risk-taking history? ______________________________

What fear has been the most influential in my financial decisions? ______________________________

What confidence has served me well? ______________________________

If my past risk decisions were data, what story do they tell about me? ______________________________

EXERCISE 3.4: THE DECISION FRAMEWORK

A Four-Part Process for Faith-Informed Risk Assessment

PART 1: INFORMATION AVAILABLE – DUE DILIGENCE

Before any significant financial decision, gather and document what you know.

Decision under consideration: ________________________________

What facts/data do I have? ________________________________

What expertise can I consult? (Advisors, mentors, trusted sources): ________________________________

What similar situations have I (or others) experienced? ________________________________

What don't I know that I could reasonably learn? ____

What information is simply unknowable? ______________________________________

On a scale of 1-10, how informed am I? ____ (1 = flying blind, 10 = all possible data gathered)

One additional source I will consult before deciding: ____

PART 2: WORST-CASE SCENARIO – FEAR INTERROGATION

Confront the worst outcome directly. Do not avoid it.

What is the absolute worst that could happen if I take this risk? ____

How likely is this worst case? ☐ Remote ☐ Unlikely ☐ Possible ☐ Likely

What would the actual consequences be? ____

Could I survive it? ☐ Yes ☐ With difficulty ☐ No

What resources would I have even in the worst case? ____

How long would recovery take? ____

What would I learn from the failure? ____

Is this worst case something I can accept? ☐ Yes ☐ No ☐ Unsure

---

PART 3: RECOVERY PLAN – MARGIN OF SAFETY

Before taking risk, design your response if things go wrong.

If this decision fails, my immediate response will be: ____

____

My financial buffer for this risk is: ____

My emotional/support resources for this risk are: ____

____

What is my exit strategy or stop-loss point? ____

____

How will I know it's time to change course? ____

____

Who will I turn to for guidance if things go wrong? ____

____

PART 4: PRAYERFUL DISCERNMENT – WISDOM BEYOND NUMBERS

Bring the decision into your spiritual practice.

Have I acknowledged this decision before God? ☐ Yes ☐ No ☐ Not yet

What scripture, principle, or teaching speaks to this situation? ____________________

____

What does my conscience say? ____________________

____

Is this decision aligned with my values and who I want to become? ____________________

____

Am I acting from fear or from faith? ____________________

Am I acting from greed or from stewardship? ____________________

____

What would it look like to make this decision with "power, love, and a sound mind"?

____

____

Silence and Stillness:

Take 5 minutes of silence before answering: What inner stillness reveals...

____

____

____

Decision Summary

Based on this four-part framework, my decision is to:

☐ Proceed with this risk
☐ Decline this risk
☐ Modify the risk by:
____
☐ Delay decision until:
____

My reasoning, integrated across all four parts: ___________________________

Date: __________ **Signature:** ___________________

EXERCISE 3.5: PROBABILITY VS. POSSIBILITY

Taming the Catastrophizing Mind

Part A: The Possibility Trap

We often act as if any possible bad outcome is a probable bad outcome. Practice distinguishing.

Fear/Concern: ___________________________

Is this possible? ☐ Yes ☐ No ☐ Unsure

Is this probable? ☐ Highly likely ☐ Moderately likely ☐ Unlikely ☐ Very unlikely

What is the evidence for its probability? ______________________________

____

What would a rational, evidence-based person say about this risk? ______________________________

____

____

Part B: Probability Calibration Practice

Estimate the probability of these events (0-100%). Then look up the actual answer.

Event	My Estimate	Actual Probability	How Off Was I?
Chance of a US recession in any given year	____%	~15-20%	

Event	My Estimate	Actual Probability	How Off Was I?
Chance of dying in a car crash in your lifetime	____%	~1%	
Chance of a house fire per year	____%	~0.5%	
Chance of losing money in the S&P 500 over any 20-year period	____%	0% (has never happened)	
Chance of being audited by the IRS	____%	~0.4%	

What does this reveal about your tendency to overestimate or underestimate risk?

____

____

EXERCISE 3.6: FEAR, GREED, AND WISDOM – THREE VOICES IN YOUR HEAD

Discerning Your Inner Council

Part A: Identifying the Voices

Think of a current financial decision you're wrestling with. Write what each "voice" says.

Decision: ____

The Voice of FEAR says:

"I'm afraid that..."

____

"You'll regret it if..."

____

"Remember when..."

____

"The safe thing is to..."

____

The Voice of GREED says:

"You could have so much more if..."

____

"Everyone else is..."

____

"This is your chance to..."

____

"Don't miss out on..."

____

____

The Voice of WISDOM says:

"Consider both what you've heard, and now reflect:"

What are the facts? ______________________________________

What are my values? ______________________________________

What is the right thing to do, not just the profitable thing? ______________________________________

What would I be proud of in 10 years? ______________________________________

What would love require? ______________________________________

Part B: Discernment Practice

Which voice is loudest right now? ☐ Fear ☐ Greed ☐ Wisdom

What would it take to give Wisdom the deciding vote? ____

EXERCISE 3.7: MARGIN OF SAFETY – BUILDING YOUR BUFFER

The Antidote to Reckless Risk

The Principle: A margin of safety is the gap between what you *expect* to happen and what you can *survive* happening. It is the foundation of wise risk-taking.

Part A: Financial Margin Audit

Area	**Current Buffer**	**Target Buffer**	**Action Needed**
Emergency fund (months of expenses)	____ months	3-6 months	
Investment diversification (single stock concentration)	____% of portfolio	<10% per position	
Debt-to-income ratio	____%	<36%	
Insurance coverage (life, disability, health)	☐ Adequate?	Review annually	
Career/income diversification	☐ Single source	Multiple streams	

Part B: Psychological Margin Audit

Area	Current Capacity	What Would Strengthen This?
Ability to handle market volatility without panic		
Confidence in my ability to earn/recover		
Support system for financial stress		
Knowledge/understanding of my investments		
Trust in my decision-making process		

Part C: Margin of Safety Statement

Based on the above, I commit to the following margin of safety principles:

1. I will not invest in anything I cannot explain in simple terms.
2. I will maintain a minimum of ____ months of essential expenses in liquid reserves.
3. I will limit any single investment to no more than ____% of my portfolio.
4. Before taking a significant risk, I will ensure my recovery plan is in place.
5. ______________________________
6. ______________________________

EXERCISE 3.8: FAITH AND RISK – THEOLOGICAL REFLECTION

What Does It Mean to Trust God With Money?

Part A: Scripture Inventory

Read each passage and reflect: What does this teach about risk, provision, and trust?

Scripture	What This Teaches Me About Risk and Faith
Proverbs 3:5-6 – "Trust in the Lord with all your heart, and lean not on your own understanding; in all your ways acknowledge Him, and He shall direct your paths."	
Matthew 25:14-30 – The Parable of the Talents (the servant who buried his money was rebuked)	
1 Timothy 6:17-19 – "Command those who are rich... not to be arrogant nor to put their hope in wealth... to do good, to be rich in good deeds, and to be generous and willing to share."	
Luke 14:28-30 – "Suppose one of you wants to build a tower. Won't you first sit down and estimate the cost to see if you have enough money to complete it?"	

Scripture	What This Teaches Me About Risk and Faith
Ecclesiastes 11:1-2 – "Ship your grain across the sea; after many days you may receive a return. Invest in seven ventures, yes, in eight; you do not know what disaster may come upon the land."	

Part B: Faith vs. Presumption

Faith trusts God while using wisdom. Presumption expects God to override foolishness.

Where is the line between faith and presumption in my financial thinking?

Faith Sounds Like...	Presumption Sounds Like...
"I will make a prudent plan and trust God with the outcome."	"I don't need to plan; God will provide."

Faith Sounds Like...	**Presumption Sounds Like...**

Am I currently using "faith" to avoid responsible planning? ☐ Yes ☐ No ☐ Unsure

Am I currently using "wisdom" to avoid trusting God? ☐ Yes ☐ No ☐ Unsure

---

Part C: My Faith-Risk Integration Statement

Complete in your own words.

I believe God calls me to be:
☐ A steward, not an owner ☐ A risk-taker for His purposes ☐ A prudent planner ☐ A generous giver

Therefore, when I face financial uncertainty, I will:

1. ______________________________
2. ______________________________
3. ______________________________

And I will trust God with: ____

EXERCISE 3.9: THE REGRET PRE-MORTEM – 20/20 FORESIGHT

Making Decisions Your Future Self Will Thank You For

Imagine it is 10 years from now. This decision did NOT go well.

Decision under consideration: ________________________________

It is now 10 years later, and this decision failed. Why?

1. ________________________________
2. ________________________________
3. ________________________________

What did I miss at the time? ____

What would I tell my younger self to do differently? ___

Now imagine it is 10 years from now. This decision went BETTER than expected.

Why did it succeed? ___

What did I do right? ___

What would I tell my younger self to do the same? ___

Integration:

What one change to my current plan does this exercise suggest? ____________________________________

BEHAVIORAL PRACTICE: 7-DAY UNCERTAINTY TOLERANCE EXPERIMENT

Experiment Choice:

☐ **Practice #1: The Information Pause** – Make one decision this week with 80% of the information you'd normally want. Notice the discomfort. Did you survive?

☐ **Practice #2: Worst-Case Visualization** – Each day, identify one financial fear and spend 2 minutes visualizing the worst case—and your survival of it.

☐ **Practice #3: The Margin Builder** – Take one concrete action to increase your financial or psychological margin of safety.

☐ **Practice #4: The Faith Declaration** – Each morning, state aloud: "I have done my part. The outcome belongs to God."

Daily Log

Day	Practice	What I Noticed	Discomfort Level (1-10)	What I Learned
1				
2				
3				
4				
5				
6				
7				

End-of-Week Reflection

What did I learn about my relationship with uncertainty? ____

What was the hardest part? ________________________________

What surprised me? ________________________________

One thing I will carry forward: ________________________________

FAITH INTEGRATION

Prayerful Discernment Practice

Scripture for Meditation

"*Commit your works to the Lord, and your thoughts will be established.*" (Proverbs 16:3)

The ACTS Framework for Financial Discernment

A – ADORATION
Begin by focusing on God, not the decision.
"*Lord, You are the owner of all things. I am a steward.*"

Write a brief prayer of adoration:

C – CONFESSION
Acknowledge where fear, greed, or foolishness have influenced you.
"*I confess that I have...*"

T – THANKSGIVING
Express gratitude for what you already have.
"*I thank You for...*"

S – SUPPLICATION

Present your request for wisdom and clarity.

"Lord, I need wisdom regarding..."

"Give me courage to act when I should, patience to wait when I should, and humility to seek counsel when I should."

Amen.

CHAPTER 3 ACTION PLAN

One risk I will take this month (with margin of safety):

One risk I will decline this month (with clarity):

One margin of safety I will strengthen:

One decision I will bring through the four-part framework:

One truth to remember:

"Faith is not the absence of uncertainty. Faith is acting on wisdom and trust when uncertainty remains."

CHAPTER 3 COMPLETION CHECKLIST

☐ I have completed my Risk Profile Assessment
☐ I have distinguished between risk and uncertainty in my current situation
☐ I have reviewed past risks and extracted lessons
☐ I have practiced the four-part decision framework
☐ I have identified my margin of safety gaps
☐ I have completed the theological reflection on faith vs. presumption
☐ I have conducted a regret pre-mortem

☐ I have completed the 7-day behavioral experiment
☐ I am ready to proceed to Chapter 4

Date Completed: ____________________________________

My Key Insight from Chapter 3:

"You cannot control the outcome. You can control the process, the margin of safety, and the intention of your heart. That is enough. That is stewardship. That is faith."

CHAPTER 04

Wealth, Success, and Identity

Separating Your Net Worth from Your Self-Worth

Learning Objectives

☐ Separate self-worth from net worth through conscious reflection
☐ Examine and deconstruct cultural definitions of success
☐ Anchor identity in values, relationships, and purpose beyond money
☐ Recognize and dismantle the comparison trap
☐ Develop a personal, authentic definition of a life well-lived

Key Concepts Review

Term	Definition	In My Own Words
Hedonic Treadmill	The tendency to return to a stable happiness baseline after positive or negative events, requiring ever-greater achievements to maintain satisfaction	
Social Comparison Theory	The drive to evaluate ourselves by comparing to others; can be upward (to those better off) or downward (to those worse off)	
Materialism	The value system focused on acquiring possessions and wealth as a path to happiness and social status	

Term	Definition	In My Own Words
Experiential Wealth	The accumulated memories, skills, and personal growth from experiences rather than possessions	
Self-Worth Contingency	Basing self-esteem on outcomes in a specific domain (e.g., financial success, appearance, approval)	
Enough	The psychologically grounded sense of sufficiency; the antidote to endless accumulation	
Eudaimonia	Aristotelian concept of flourishing through virtue and meaningful activity, not mere pleasure	

Term	Definition	In My Own Words
Legacy Identity	The self-concept rooted in what you contribute and leave behind, not what you accumulate	

EXERCISE 4.1: IDENTITY AND MONEY – THE DEEP CONNECTION

Uncovering Where Self-Worth Meets Net Worth

Part A: Sentence Completion – Your First, Honest Answers

Complete each sentence with your immediate, unfiltered response.

I feel successful when:

____

Money makes me feel valuable when: ____

If I lost all my money tomorrow, I would still be: ____

When I compare myself to others financially, I usually feel: ____

The thing I fear people would think if they knew my full financial picture is: ____

I would describe my current relationship between my self-worth and my net worth as:

☐ Completely separate ☐ Somewhat connected ☐ Deeply entangled ☐ I don't know

Part B: The Worth Audit

For each domain, rate how much your self-worth depends on it (1 = not at all, 5 = completely).

Domain	Dependency (1-5)
My income level	
My savings/investment balance	
My possessions (home, car, etc.)	
My job title/career status	
My ability to provide for family	
My generosity/giving	
My financial knowledge/competence	
My appearance/status symbols	
My relationships	

Domain	Dependency (1-5)
My character/integrity	
My contributions to others	
My spiritual/faith life	

Rank your top three sources of self-worth:

1. ______
2. ______
3. ______

Rank your top three sources of financial anxiety:

1. ______
2. ______
3. ______

What connections do you notice between these lists? ______

______

______

Part C: The "If/Then" Identity Trap

Complete these statements honestly.

I believe that IF I have [financial goal/possession/status], THEN I will feel [emotion/identity].

If I have ______________________________, then I will feel

____.

If I have ______________________________, then I will feel

____.

If I have ______________________________, then I will feel

____.

Now, reflect on a past goal you achieved.

A financial/status goal I once achieved was:

____

Before achieving it, I believed it would make me feel:

____

After achieving it, I actually felt:

____

What does this tell you about the connection between achievement and identity?

EXERCISE 4.2: THE COMPARISON TRAP – MAPPING YOUR SOCIAL REFERENCE POINTS

Who Are the Joneses in Your Life?

Part A: Reference Group Identification

List the people or groups you unconsciously compare yourself to financially.

Person/Group	Relationship	Domain of Comparison (e.g., income, home, lifestyle)	Effect on Me (Emotion/Behavior)
Example: College roommate	Former peer	Career success, travel	Envy, urge to overspend on vacations
1.			
2.			
3.			

Person/Group	Relationship	Domain of Comparison (e.g., income, home, lifestyle)	Effect on Me (Emotion/Behavior)
4.			
5.			
6. (Social media influencers)			
7. (Fictional ideal)			

Part B: The Cost of Comparison

What has this comparison cost me financially?

☐ Lifestyle inflation ☐ Unnecessary purchases ☐ Investment FOMO ☐ Career dissatisfaction ☐ Debt ☐ Other: _______

Estimated financial cost (if quantifiable): $__________

What has this comparison cost me emotionally/spiritually?

☐ Chronic dissatisfaction ☐ Envy/resentment ☐ Shame ☐ Anxiety ☐ Loss of gratitude ☐ Damaged relationships ☐ Other: ___________________________

Part C: Upward vs. Downward Comparison

Upward comparison (to those with more):
Whom do I look up to financially?

____

How does this motivate me?

____

How does this discourage me?

____

Downward comparison (to those with less):
When I consider those with less financial security, I feel:

____

Is this gratitude or condescension? ☐ Gratitude ☐ Condescension ☐ Mixed

Healthy reference shift:
Who is someone I admire for their *character* or *peace* rather than their *possessions*?

What would it mean to make them my primary reference point? ____

____

____

Part D: Social Media Audit

Platforms I use most: ☐ Instagram ☐ Facebook ☐ LinkedIn ☐ TikTok ☐ Twitter/X ☐ Other: _____

Accounts that trigger financial comparison/envy: ____

____

Accounts that inspire healthy financial values: ____

____

One account I will unfollow/mute this week: ____

One account I will follow for healthier perspective: ____

My social media intention: ____

EXERCISE 4.3: CULTURAL DEFINITIONS OF SUCCESS – DECONSTRUCTING THE SCRIPT

Whose Life Are You Living?

Part A: The Cultural Success Inventory

What messages have you absorbed about what "success" looks like?

Source	Message About Success
My family of origin	
My school/education	
My workplace/profession	
Media/TV/Movies	

Source	Message About Success
Social media	
Religious community	
Peers/friends	
Advertising	

The dominant cultural definition of success I've internalized is:

On a scale of 1-10, how much does this definition actually reflect what I deeply value?

1 ☐ 2 ☐ 3 ☐ 4 ☐ 5 ☐ 6 ☐ 7 ☐ 8 ☐ 9 ☐ 10 ☐ (1 = not at all, 10 = completely)

Part B: The "Should" Audit

Complete these sentences with the cultural "shoulds" you hear in your head.

By now, I should have:

____

A successful person should:

____

If I were really successful, I would:

____

People would respect me more if I:

____

I'll feel like I've "made it" when:

____

Where did each "should" come from? _________________________________

Which of these "shoulds" do I want to keep? ____________________________

Which do I want to release? ____

Part C: Redefining Success – Your Personal Success Manifesto

Rewrite "success" using your own values, not cultural possessions.

Success is not: ____

Success is: ____

____

A successful life, to me, looks like: ________________________________

____

____

What I want to be remembered for: ________________________________

____

The measure of success I want to track: ______________________________

____

____

EXERCISE 4.4: MATERIALISM VS. EXPERIENTIAL WEALTH

Where Your Money Actually Buys Happiness

Part A: The Purchase Retrospective

Think of three significant purchases you've made in the past year.

Purchase	Cost	Happiness at Purchase (1-10)	Happiness Now (1-10)	Why Did It Fade or Endure?
1.				
2.				
3.				

Think of three significant experiences you've funded.

Experience	Cost	Happiness at Time (1-10)	Happiness Now (Memory) (1-10)	Why Does It Endure?
1.				
2.				
3.				

What patterns do you notice? ______________________________

____

____

Part B: The Experience Advantage – Personal Evidence

A memory of an experience that has become part of my identity: ____________

____

A possession that faded into the background: ______________________

One experience I will invest in this year: ______________________________

Why this experience aligns with my values: ___________________________

Part C: The "Experience Portfolio" – Diversifying Your Joy

Use this table to plan a balanced portfolio of experiences across different need categories.

Category	Need Met	Past Experience I Loved	Future Experience I Want
Social/Connection	Relatedness, belonging		

Category	Need Met	Past Experience I Loved	Future Experience I Want
Challenge/Growth	Competence, mastery		
Novelty/Awe	Wonder, perspective		
Restoration/Peace	Calm, recharging		
Contribution/Service	Purpose, generativity		

My commitment: I will allocate $_______ per month/year to my "Experience Portfolio."

Funding source: ☐ Reallocate from material spending ☐ New income ☐ Savings ☐ Other

EXERCISE 4.5: THE HEDONIC TREADMILL – STEPPING OFF

Escaping the "Never Enough" Cycle

Part A: Treadmill Recognition

A possession or achievement I once desperately wanted, now feels ordinary:

What I believed it would give me: ______________________________

What it actually gave me: ______________________________

Another area where I notice the "treadmill" effect: ______________________________

Part B: The "Enough" Question

Answer these questions slowly and honestly.

How much money is enough to:

- Feel secure? $___________
- Meet my basic needs with dignity? $___________
- Enjoy life without constant financial stress? $___________
- Be generous in ways that matter to me? $___________
- Never have to work for money again? $___________

If I had that "enough" amount, what would be different about my life? _______

What would still be the same? ____

What would still need to be addressed that money cannot solve? ____

Part C: Intermittent Deprivation – Resetting the Treadmill

Choose one practice to reset your adaptation.

☐ **No-Spend Week:** One week with zero non-essential purchases. Observe cravings and satisfaction.

☐ **Digital Fast:** 48 hours with no social media or financial apps. Notice comparison urges.

☐ **Simplicity Meal:** Eat only basic, inexpensive meals for 3 days. Appreciate the next meal out.

☐ **Possession Pause:** Remove half your clothing from your closet for 2 weeks. See what you miss.

My chosen reset practice: ______________________________

Planned dates: ____________________ to ____________________

What I hope to learn: ______________________________

EXERCISE 4.6: ANCHORING IDENTITY BEYOND MONEY

Who Are You When You Take Away the Numbers?

Part A: The Identity Deconstruction

Imagine you lost your job, your savings, your home, and all your possessions tomorrow. Answer these questions from that stripped-down place.

My name is: ______________________________

I am still: ______________________________

____

I am good at: ______________________________

____

People who love me would say I am: ______________________________

____

I believe in: ______________________________

____

I can contribute: ______________________________

My life still has meaning because: ______________________

What does this exercise reveal about your core, non-financial self? ______________________

Part B: The Eulogy Exercise

At your funeral, what do you want people to say about you? Not your resume. Your character.

My partner/spouse would say: ______________________

My children/family would say: ______________________

My faith community would say: ______________________

The words I most want spoken about me: ______________________

How am I investing in becoming that person today? ____

Part C: Identity Portfolio – Diversifying Your Self-Concept

Rate your current investment in each identity domain (1 = minimal, 5 = primary focus).

Identity Domain	Current Investment (1-5)	Desired Investment (1-5)	One Action to Shift
Professional/Occupational			
Family/Relational			
Community/Civic			

Identity Domain	Current Investment (1-5)	Desired Investment (1-5)	One Action to Shift
Creative/Expressive			
Intellectual/Learning			
Spiritual/Philosophical			
Physical/Health			
Hobbyist/Recreational			

Reflection: If I over-invest in one domain, what am I neglecting? ______________________________

____

What is the risk of that neglect? ______________________________

____

One identity domain I will intentionally develop this year: ______________________________

My first step: ______________________________

EXERCISE 4.7: GENEROSITY AND IDENTITY

Finding Yourself by Giving Yourself Away

Part A: The Generosity Inventory

Think of a time you gave money, time, or resources to someone else.

What did you give? ______________________________

How did it feel during the act? ______________________________

How did it feel afterward? ______________________________

What did this experience teach you about yourself? ______________________________

Part B: Identity Through Generosity

Complete these sentences.

I am the kind of person who gives to:

____

Giving makes me feel:

____

If I were more generous with my resources, I would:

____

One fear I have about giving more:

____

One belief I need to release to become more generous:

____

Part C: A Generosity Experiment

This month, I will give (circle one):
☐ Money ☐ Time ☐ Skill ☐ Attention ☐ Hospitality

To/For: ____

My intention for this experiment: ____

Post-Experiment Reflection:

What I gave:

____

How it felt:

____

What I learned about myself:

____

How this affected my sense of identity/wealth:

____

EXERCISE 4.8: THE STEALTH WEALTH PRACTICE

Finding Peace in Inconspicuous Sufficiency

The Principle: True financial freedom is the ability to live well without needing to display it.

Part A: Stealth Wealth Self-Assessment

Statement	True	False	I'm Working on It
I feel pressure to display my success through possessions.	☐	☐	☐
I derive private satisfaction from living below my means.	☐	☐	☐
I worry that people will judge me if I don't have certain things.	☐	☐	☐
I have a clear sense of "enough" for my lifestyle.	☐	☐	☐
I can enjoy quality without needing recognizable brands.	☐	☐	☐

Statement	True	False	I'm Working on It
My security is more important than my status signals.	☐	☐	☐

Part B: Inconspicuous Consumption Planning

Where can you shift spending from public display to private meaning?

Area of Spending	Current (Conspicuous)	Desired (Inconspicuous)	Private Joy I Would Gain
Vehicle			
Home			
Clothing			
Dining/Entertainment			

Area of Spending	Current (Conspicuous)	Desired (Inconspicuous)	Private Joy I Would Gain
Travel			
Hobbies			

Part C: My Stealth Wealth Statement

Complete this personal manifesto.

I choose to live below my means not because I cannot afford more, but because:

I take private pleasure in: ____

My security is a quiet confidence, not a public announcement.

My freedom is more valuable than my status.

BEHAVIORAL PRACTICE: 7-DAY IDENTITY AND COMPARISON EXPERIMENT

Experiment Choice (choose one):

☐ **Experiment A: The Comparison Fast** – For 7 days, consciously avoid all financial comparison. Unfollow triggers. When comparison thoughts arise, gently redirect.

☐ **Experiment B: The Experience Investment** – Spend money on ONE meaningful experience this week. Journal before, during, and after.

☐ **Experiment C: The Gratitude Anchor** – Each day, write three non-financial things you value about yourself.

☐ **Experiment D: The Generosity Act** – Perform one anonymous act of financial generosity. Do not tell anyone. Journal the experience.

Daily Log

Day	Experiment Activity	What I Noticed	Emotions	Insights
1				
2				
3				
4				
5				
6				
7				

End-of-Week Reflection

What was the most powerful moment of this experiment? ________________________________

What did I learn about my attachment to money/status? ___________________________

What did I learn about my identity beyond money? ___________________________

One practice I will continue: ___________________________

FAITH INTEGRATION

Your Worth Before God and the World

Scripture Meditation

"And He said to them, 'Take care, and be on your guard against all covetousness, for one's life does not consist in the abundance of his possessions.'" (Luke 12:15)

"Charm is deceitful, and beauty is vain, but a woman who fears the Lord is to be praised." (Proverbs 31:30)

"But far be it from me to boast except in the cross of our Lord Jesus Christ." (Galatians 6:14)

Part A: Theological Reflection on Worth

According to my faith, where does my true worth come from? ______________________________

____

What does God see when He looks at me? ______________________________

____

How does this contrast with how the world measures worth? ______________________________

____

What would change if I truly believed my worth is God-given, not earned? ______________________________

____

____

Part B: Prayer of Release

Write a prayer releasing your identity from financial performance.

____

____

____

____

____

Part C: Identity Affirmation

Speak this aloud (or silently) daily.

"I am not my net worth. I am not my job title. I am not my possessions.

I am a child of God, created in His image, loved unconditionally.

My value is not determined by my bank account but by my Creator.

I am free to steward money without being defined by it.

I am enough, right now, not because of what I have, but because of Whose I am."

CHAPTER 4 ACTION PLAN

One cultural definition of success I will consciously reject:

One personal definition of success I will consciously embrace:

One comparison trigger I will eliminate or reduce:

One identity domain I will invest in this month (beyond money):

One experience I will fund over one possession:

One truth to remember:

"Life does not consist in the abundance of possessions." (Luke 12:15)

CHAPTER 4 COMPLETION CHECKLIST

☐ I have completed the Identity Mapping exercise
☐ I have identified my primary comparison targets and their costs
☐ I have written my personal definition of success
☐ I have compared material vs. experiential purchases
☐ I have reflected on my "enough" number
☐ I have completed the identity deconstruction exercise
☐ I have drafted a eulogy or legacy statement
☐ I have completed the 7-day behavioral experiment
☐ I have engaged with the faith integration reflection
☐ I am ready to proceed to Chapter 5

Date Completed: ____

My Key Insight from Chapter 4:

"The most important wealth is not in your portfolio, but in your heart, your mind, your body, and your community. You begin to measure your wealth not by what you have in your bank, but by what you have in your soul."

CHAPTER 05

Time, Patience, and Compounding

The Hidden Power of Waiting

Learning Objectives

☐ Understand the psychology of delayed gratification and its financial impact
☐ Identify personal time horizons and how they shape decisions
☐ Recognize present bias and hyperbolic discounting in daily choices
☐ Calculate the long-term effects of small, consistent actions
☐ Develop practices to strengthen patience and long-term thinking

☐ Cultivate a generational perspective beyond your own lifetime

---

Key Concepts Review

Term	**Definition**	**In My Own Words**
Compounding	The exponential growth of an asset when earnings are reinvested to generate their own earnings over time	
Delayed Gratification	The ability to resist an immediate reward in favor of a larger or more enduring later reward	
Time Horizon	The length of time over which an investment or financial plan is expected	

Term	Definition	In My Own Words
	to be held before liquidation	
Present Bias (Hyperbolic Discounting)	The tendency to overvalue immediate rewards at the expense of future rewards; the discount rate decreases over time	
Future Self	The psychological concept of one's identity projected forward; the degree of connection to future self influences saving behavior	
Marshmallow Test	Classic Stanford experiment on delayed gratification in children;	

Term	Definition	In My Own Words
	correlated with long-term life outcomes	
Sequence of Returns Risk	The danger that investment losses occur early in retirement, devastating long-term portfolio sustainability	
Intergenerational Wealth	Financial and non-financial capital passed to future generations; requires multi-decade thinking	

EXERCISE 5.1: TIME HORIZON SELF-ASSESSMENT

What Lens Do You Use?

Part A: Your Default Time Frame

When I think about my financial life, I usually focus on:

☐ **Days** – What I need right now, today's expenses, immediate cravings
☐ **Months** – This month's bills, the next few paychecks, short-term goals
☐ **Years** – Next year's vacation, a car in 3 years, saving for a home
☐ **Decades** – Retirement, children's education, long-term investments
☐ **Generations** – Legacy, inheritance, family wealth, impact beyond my life

Has this time horizon changed over your life? ☐ Yes ☐ No ☐ Unsure

If yes, what shifted it? ____

Part B: Time Horizon by Domain

Different financial decisions may have different time horizons. Rate your typical focus for each.

Domain	Days	Months	Years	Decades	Generations
Daily spending decisions	☐	☐	☐	☐	☐
Saving for emergencies	☐	☐	☐	☐	☐
Investing in retirement	☐	☐	☐	☐	☐
Career/income growth	☐	☐	☐	☐	☐
Major purchases (home, car)	☐	☐	☐	☐	☐
Education (self or children)	☐	☐	☐	☐	☐

Domain	Days	Months	Years	Decades	Generations
Philanthropy/giving	☐	☐	☐	☐	☐
Estate planning/legacy	☐	☐	☐	☐	☐

Where do you tend to think shortest? ______________________________

Where do you tend to think longest? ______________________________

What would change if you extended your time horizon in one domain? ______________________________

Part C: The Generations Test

Imagine your great-grandchild, 100 years from now. What financial decision you make today might still affect them?

Do you currently consider this perspective when making financial choices?

☐ Often ☐ Sometimes ☐ Rarely ☐ Never

What would it mean to start thinking like a generational steward, not just a lifetime owner?

EXERCISE 5.2: PATIENCE INVENTORY

Where Do You Rush?

Part A: Impatience Triggers

List situations where you feel the urge to rush a financial outcome.

Situation	What I Typically Do	Emotional Driver	Typical Outcome
Example: Waiting for an investment to recover	**I sell at the bottom**	**Fear of further loss**	**Locked in loss**
1.			
2.			
3.			
4.			
5.			

Pattern I notice: ____

One area where impatience has cost me the most: ____

____

Part B: The Patience Cost Calculator

Think of one specific financial decision you rushed.

Decision: ______________________________

What I did: ______________________________

What I wish I had done: ______________________________

Estimated financial cost: $______________________________

Estimated emotional cost: ______________________________

What I learned: ______________________________

Part C: The Waiting Success Story

Think of a time when waiting paid off – financially or otherwise.

What I waited for: ______________________________

How long I waited: ______________________________

What made waiting difficult: ______________________________

What helped me wait: ____

The outcome: ____

What this experience taught me about myself: ____

____

____

EXERCISE 5.3: THE COMPOUND EFFECT – SEEING THE INVISIBLE

Small, Consistent Actions × Time = Extraordinary Results

Part A: The Rule of 72

The Rule of 72: Divide 72 by your annual rate of return to estimate years to double your money.

If I earn ____% annually, my money doubles every ____ years.

If I start with $10,000 at age 25 and earn 7% annually, at age 65 I will have: $_______

(Use calculator or formula: 10,000 × (1.07)^40 ≈ $149,744)

If I start at age 35 instead: $______ *(≈ $76,123)*

If I start at age 45 instead: $______ *(≈ $38,697)*

What does this reveal about the value of time? ____

____

____

Part B: The Latte Factor – Your Personal Compounding Levers

Small, regular amounts compound into significant sums. Identify your own.

Daily/Weekly Expense	Amount	If Invested Monthly for 30 Years at 7%	Total
Example: Daily coffee	$4.50	$135/month	~$155,000
1.			

Daily/Weekly Expense	Amount	If Invested Monthly for 30 Years at 7%	Total
2.			
3.			
4.			

One small expense I could redirect toward my future self: ______________________________

Amount per month: $________

Projected value in 30 years at 7%: $________ *(Use online calculator or rough estimate: monthly × 12 × (1.07^30 - 1)/0.07)*

Part C: Visualizing the Curve

Sketch or describe the difference between linear and exponential growth.

Linear growth looks like: ______________________________

Exponential growth looks like: ____

Where in my financial life have I experienced the "bend in the curve" – the point where compounding becomes visible?

Where am I still in the flat part of the curve, needing patience? ____________________________________

EXERCISE 5.4: DELAYED GRATIFICATION – THE MARSHMALLOW TEST FOR ADULTS

What Helps You Wait?

Part A: Your Waiting Strategies

When you successfully delay gratification, what helps you? (Check all that apply)

☐ Visualizing the future reward vividly
☐ Reminding myself of my long-term goals
☐ Distracting myself with another activity
☐ Making the immediate reward less accessible (friction)
☐ Public commitment / accountability
☐ Thinking about my future self
☐ Breaking the wait into smaller chunks
☐ Faith / prayer / spiritual practice
☐ Other:

____

Your most effective strategy: ______________________________________

Part B: The Future Self Continuum

Psychologists find that people who feel more connected to their future selves save more.

On a scale of 1-10, how connected do you feel to your "65-year-old self"?

1 ☐ 2 ☐ 3 ☐ 4 ☐ 5 ☐ 6 ☐ 7 ☐ 8 ☐ 9 ☐ 10 ☐
(1 = "A stranger," 10 = "Clearly me, just older")

Close your eyes and imagine your future self at age 70. What do they look like? How do they move? What do they care about?

What would your future self thank you for doing today? ____

What would your future self forgive you for, but wish you had started sooner? ______________________________

Part C: The Immediacy Temptation Log

Over the next 3 days, log every time you feel the pull of "I want it now."

Time	What I Wanted	Immediate Reward	Long-Term Goal It Conflicts With	What I Did

Patterns I notice: ____

EXERCISE 5.5: PRESENT BIAS – RECOGNIZING THE TYRANNY OF NOW

Why Tomorrow Always Seems Less Important

Part A: The Discounting Dilemma

Answer honestly.

Would you prefer:

☐ $100 today OR ☐ $120 in one month?

☐ $100 today OR ☐ $150 in one year?

☐ $100 in one year OR ☐ $120 in one year and one month?

What do your answers reveal? ____

Most people take the $100 today even though waiting one month yields 20% return. But when both options are delayed, patience increases. This is hyperbolic discounting.

Part B: Personal Discount Rate

How much would you need to be paid to wait?

I would wait 1 year for $100 today if the future amount were at least $________

What does this imply about your "personal discount rate"? ________________

(Example: If you require $120, your annual discount rate is 20%.)

How does this rate compare to stock market returns (~7-10%)? ________________

What decisions in your life reflect this high discount rate? ________________

Part C: Precommitment – Tying Yourself to the Mast

Like Ulysses tying himself to resist the Sirens, we can bind our future selves to wise choices.

What precommitment devices do you already use? ____

One new precommitment I will implement:

☐ Automate savings/investments so money is gone before I can spend it
☐ Enroll in auto-escalation for retirement contributions
☐ Use a "cooling-off" rule for online purchases
☐ Tell someone my goal to create accountability
☐ Use a commitment app (e.g., StickK) with financial penalty
☐ Other:

____

My precommitment statement:

"I, ________________, commit to ________________ by ________________. To increase my chances of success, I will ________________."

EXERCISE 5.6: GENERATIONAL THINKING – BEYOND YOUR LIFETIME

Planting Trees You Will Never Sit Under

Part A: The Legacy Question

"Society grows great when old men plant trees whose shade they know they shall never sit in." – Greek proverb

What "trees" have been planted for you by previous generations?

☐ Financial inheritance ☐ Education funded ☐ Values/faith ☐ Work ethic ☐ Home/Property ☐ Other: ____________________

How has this shaped your life? ____

____

What "trees" are you planting now that you may never sit under? ____

____

What would you like to leave for the next generation – beyond money? ____

____

____

Part B: Generational Time Horizon Exercise

Imagine writing a letter to your great-grandchild, to be opened 80 years from now.

What would you want them to know about you? ____

What values would you want them to carry? ________________________________

What financial wisdom would you pass down? ________________________________

How does this perspective change how you view today's financial decisions? ________________________________

Part C: The Multi-Generational Stewardship Plan

I currently have:

☐ A will ☐ A trust ☐ Beneficiary designations ☐ Estate plan ☐ None of these

I have communicated my estate plan to my heirs: ☐ Yes ☐ No ☐ Partially

I have shared the "why" behind my wealth with my family: ☐ Yes ☐ No ☐ Not yet

One step I will take this year toward generational stewardship: ______________________________

EXERCISE 5.7: THE COST OF IMPATIENCE – A FINANCIAL POST-MORTEM

What Impatience Has Cost You

Part A: Transaction Costs of Frequent Trading

If you trade investments frequently, estimate your costs.

Cost Type	Estimated Annual Amount
Commissions/fees	$

Cost Type	Estimated Annual Amount
Bid-ask spreads	$
Short-term capital gains tax (higher rate)	$
Underperformance vs. buy-and-hold	$
Total Estimated Cost of Impatience	**$**

Reflection: What could this money have become in 20 years at 7%? $______________________________________

Part B: Timing the Market – The Penalty Box

Have you ever:
☐ Sold investments during a downturn out of fear?
☐ Waited to invest, trying to time the bottom?
☐ Jumped into a "hot" investment at its peak?
☐ Switched strategies frequently based on recent performance?

What did this cost you? ____

_

What did you learn? ____

Part C: Non-Financial Costs of Impatience

What has impatience cost you in:

Relationships: ____

____

Peace of mind: ____

Health/stress: ____

____

Opportunities for growth: ____

Other: ____

____

EXERCISE 5.8: BUILDING PATIENCE MUSCLES – DAILY PRACTICES

Training for Long-Term Thinking

Part A: Patience Practices

Choose 2-3 practices to incorporate into your routine.

☐ **The 24-Hour Rule** – For any non-essential purchase over $X, wait 24 hours. Journal the urge.

☐ **The "One-Year Letter"** – When you want to make a major financial change, write a letter to your future self explaining why. Read it in one year.

☐ **Market Downturn Ritual** – When markets drop, read your Investment Policy Statement instead of your portfolio.

☐ **Future Self Visualization** – Spend 2 minutes daily imagining your retired self, feeling grateful for your patience.

☐ **The Slow Reading Habit** – Read one long-form financial book or article per month, resisting the urge to skim.

☐ **Generational Journal** – Keep a journal of wisdom, stories, and values to pass down.

☐ **Nature Exposure** – Spend time in natural environments that operate on slow, invisible timescales (forests, oceans, mountains).

Part B: My Patience Training Plan

Practice 1: ____

When/How often: ____

Practice 2: ____

When/How often: ____

Practice 3: ____

When/How often: ____

How will I track my progress? ______________________________

BEHAVIORAL PRACTICE: 7-DAY PATIENCE EXPERIMENT

Experiment Choice (choose one):

☐ **Experiment A: The Waiting Practice** – For 7 days, whenever you want something (purchase, checking account, acting on impulse), wait at least 1 hour. Journal the experience.

☐ **Experiment B: The Compounding Visualizer** – Each day, calculate the 30-year future value of a small amount you saved or didn't spend that day. Write it down.

☐ **Experiment C: Future Self Letter** – Write a letter from your 70-year-old self to your current self. Read it each morning.

☐ **Experiment D: The "No-Look" Week** – Do not check investment or retirement account balances for 7 days. Observe the urge and your response.

Daily Log

Day	Experiment Activity	What I Noticed	Urge Level (1-10)	What Helped Me Wait
1				
2				
3				
4				
5				
6				
7				

End-of-Week Reflection

What was the hardest moment of waiting? ______________________________

What made waiting easier? ____________________

What did I learn about my relationship with time and money? ____________________

One waiting skill I will continue to practice: ____________________

FAITH INTEGRATION

Patience, Providence, and the Long View

Scripture Meditation

"*The plans of the diligent lead surely to abundance, but everyone who is hasty comes only to poverty.*" (Proverbs 21:5)

"*But do not overlook this one fact, beloved, that with the Lord one day is as a thousand years, and a thousand years as one day. The Lord is not slow to fulfill his promise as some count slowness...*" (2 Peter 3:8-9)

"*I waited patiently for the Lord; he inclined to me and heard my cry.*" (Psalm 40:1)

"*For everything there is a season, and a time for every matter under heaven.*" (Ecclesiastes 3:1)

Part A: Theological Reflection on Time

What does my faith teach me about waiting? ______________________________

How does God's eternal perspective challenge my impatience? ______________________________

What spiritual disciplines have helped you cultivate patience? ______________________________

How might financial patience be a form of faith? ________________________________

Part B: Prayer of Patience

Write a prayer asking for the grace to wait well.

Part C: Faith and Compounding

What are the "compounding" effects in your spiritual life?
(Small, consistent practices that yield exponential growth over time.)

Small Daily Practice	Long-Term Spiritual Fruit
Example: Morning prayer	Deeper trust, peace, perspective

What connection do you see between spiritual compounding and financial compounding?

CHAPTER 5 ACTION PLAN

One financial decision I will approach with a longer time horizon:

One impatience trigger I will prepare for:

One precommitment device I will implement:

One small, consistent action I will start to harness compounding:

One step I will take toward generational stewardship:

One truth to remember:

"Time is the friend of the wonderful company, the enemy of the mediocre." – Warren Buffett

Or

"The most powerful force in the universe is compound interest." – Albert Einstein (attributed)

CHAPTER 5 COMPLETION CHECKLIST

☐ I have completed my Time Horizon Self-Assessment
☐ I have identified where I rush financial outcomes
☐ I have calculated the compound effect of small changes
☐ I have reflected on a successful experience of delayed gratification
☐ I have recognized my present bias and personal discount rate
☐ I have considered generational thinking and legacy
☐ I have estimated the cost of impatience in my finances
☐ I have designed a patience training plan
☐ I have completed the 7-day behavioral experiment
☐ I have engaged with the faith integration reflection
☐ I am ready to proceed to Chapter 6

Date Completed: ____

My Key Insight from Chapter 5:

"The tree that grows slowly bears the best fruit. The oak that stands for centuries spent decades underground, unseen, building roots. Do not despise the hidden season. Your compounding is not yet visible, but it is happening. Wait. Trust. Continue."

CHAPTER 06

Trauma, Poverty, and Financial Healing

Reclaiming Your Sacred Relationship with Money

Learning Objectives

☐ Identify and name experiences of financial trauma and wounding

☐ Understand the psychological and neurological effects of the poverty mindset

☐ Recognize how scarcity conditioning persists even after circumstances change

☐ Begin the process of healing financial wounds with

compassion and truth

☐ Separate your financial past from your financial identity

☐ Develop practices for post-traumatic financial growth

Key Concepts Review

Term	Definition	In My Own Words
Financial Trauma	A psychological wound caused by a distressing financial event or prolonged economic deprivation that continues to affect beliefs, emotions, and behaviors	
Poverty Mindset (Scarcity Conditioning)	A set of beliefs and coping strategies formed during prolonged financial hardship; persists even when circumstances improve	

Term	Definition	In My Own Words
Scarcity Loop	The self-reinforcing cycle where perceived scarcity narrows focus, depletes cognitive bandwidth, and leads to decisions that perpetuate scarcity	
Financial Avoidance	A trauma response characterized by refusing to open statements, pay bills, or acknowledge financial reality as a form of self-protection	
Money Shame	The painful belief that financial struggles reflect a fundamental flaw in one's character or worth	
Financial Hypervigilance	A trauma response characterized by constant monitoring, inability to relax, and catastrophic worry about money	

Term	Definition	In My Own Words
Post-Traumatic Financial Growth	The positive psychological transformation that can occur when financial trauma is processed, leading to greater wisdom, resilience, and purposeful stewardship	
Financial Self-Compassion	Treating oneself with kindness, understanding, and non-judgment in response to past financial mistakes or struggles	

EXERCISE 6.1: FINANCIAL PAIN TIMELINE

Mapping Your History with Money

Part A: Creating Your Timeline

This exercise is an act of courage. Create a chronological map of significant financial experiences—both painful and positive. Take your time. You may complete this over several sessions.

Age	**Event/Experience**	**Emotion(s) Felt**	**Impact on Beliefs About Money**	**Impact on Behavior**
Example: Age 8	***Heard parents arguing about bills through the wall***	***Fear, confusion, guilt***	***"Money is dangerous." "I am a burden."***	***Stopped asking for things; became hyper-independent***

Part B: The Earliest Memory

My earliest memory of financial pain or stress is:

I was approximately ____ years old.

The emotions I felt then

were: ____

The message I internalized about money from this

experience was: ____________________________________

The message I internalized about myself from this

experience was: ____________________________________

How does this memory still show up in my adult financial

life? ____

Part C: The Body Keeps the Score

Financial trauma is not just a memory; it is stored in the body.

When I think about that early financial memory, where do I feel it in my body?

☐ Chest (tightness, heaviness)

☐ Stomach (knots, nausea)

☐ Shoulders (tension, up to ears)

☐ Jaw (clenched)

☐ Throat (lump, tightness)

☐ Other: ______________________________

When in your current financial life do you feel this same physical sensation?

What might your body be trying to tell you? ____

EXERCISE 6.2: THE POVERTY MINDSET INVENTORY

Recognizing Scarcity Conditioning

Part A: Scarcity Beliefs – Past and Present

For each belief, check if it was present in your past and if it persists today.

Belief	Was True for Me in the Past	Is Still True for Me Today
There will never be enough.	☐	☐
I have to take whatever I can get, right now.	☐	☐
Money always leaves as fast as it comes.	☐	☐

Belief	Was True for Me in the Past	Is Still True for Me Today
I don't deserve to have nice things.	☐	☐
People like me don't get ahead.	☐	☐
If I have money, someone will take it.	☐	☐
It's dangerous to let others know I have money.	☐	☐
I'll never be truly secure.	☐	☐
Financial planning is pointless because something will go wrong.	☐	☐
I'm just not good with money.	☐	☐

Which beliefs are the most deeply rooted? ______________________________

Which belief, if you could release it, would change the most? ______________________

Part B: Scarcity Behaviors – Survival Strategies

During times of financial scarcity, we develop survival strategies. Some outlive their usefulness.

Check any behaviors you developed during financial hardship:

☐ Hoarding cash even when it loses value to inflation
☐ Avoiding looking at bank accounts or bills
☐ Inability to spend on legitimate needs without guilt
☐ Impulsive "treat yourself" spending when money appears
☐ Turning down opportunities that require upfront investment
☐ Staying in toxic jobs because the income feels "safe"
☐ Difficulty trusting financial professionals
☐ Keeping financial secrets from partner/family
☐ Assuming the worst-case outcome will happen

☐ Other:

____

Which of these behaviors are still active in your life today? ____________________________________

What were they trying to protect you from? ____________________________________

What do they cost you now? ____________________________________

Part C: The Scarcity Loop – Self-Perpetuating Cycle

Draw or describe your personal scarcity loop.

Trigger (e.g., unexpected bill, market drop, comparison)

→

Feeling (e.g., fear, overwhelm, shame)

→

Thought (e.g., "See, I'll never get ahead," "This always happens to me")

→

Action (e.g., avoid, panic, hoard, splurge)

→

Outcome (e.g., missed opportunity, debt, no progress)

→

Reinforced Belief (e.g., "I was right—I can't trust money/trust myself")

→

Back to Trigger

My personal scarcity loop: ____

____

____

____

Where in this loop do I have the most power to interrupt it? ____

EXERCISE 6.3: THE TUNNEL EFFECT – WHEN SCARCITY STEALS YOUR MENTAL BANDWIDTH

Understanding the Cognitive Tax of Financial Stress

Part A: The Tunneling Experience

Sendhil Mullainathan and Eldar Shafir's research shows that scarcity creates "tunneling"—extreme focus on immediate scarcity at the expense of everything else.

Describe a time when financial stress consumed so much of your mental energy that you neglected other important areas of your life (health, relationships, planning):

What was pushed out of the tunnel? ______________________________

What decisions did you make in that tunnel that you later regretted? ______________________________

Part B: Cognitive Load Assessment

Financial stress is a tax on your mental capacity. Assess your current cognitive load.

In the past month, how often have you...	Never	Rarely	Sometimes	Often	Constantly
Felt unable to think clearly about finances?	☐	☐	☐	☐	☐
Avoided financial tasks because they felt overwhelming?	☐	☐	☐	☐	☐
Lost sleep worrying about money?	☐	☐	☐	☐	☐
Made a decision you knew was unwise because you needed immediate relief?	☐	☐	☐	☐	☐

In the past month, how often have you...	Never	Rarely	Sometimes	Often	Constantly
Felt that financial stress was affecting your work or relationships?	☐	☐	☐	☐	☐

What does this tell you about your current cognitive bandwidth? ____________________

____

What is one thing you could do to free up mental space? ____________________

____

____

EXERCISE 6.4: FINANCIAL TRAUMA TYPOLOGY

Naming the Wound

Part A: Types of Financial Trauma

Not all financial wounds look the same. Check those that apply to your history.

☐ ACUTE FINANCIAL TRAUMA – A single, catastrophic event

- Sudden job loss without warning
- Major investment loss or business failure
- Bankruptcy or foreclosure
- Destructive divorce financial settlement
- Sudden, unpayable medical debt
- Financial fraud or exploitation
- Other: ____

Describe the event: ____

☐ **CHRONIC FINANCIAL TRAUMA – Prolonged deprivation**

- Growing up in persistent poverty
- Long-term unemployment or underemployment
- Generational poverty patterns
- Years of living paycheck to paycheck
- Chronic debt that never decreases
- Other: ____
_

Describe the experience: _______________________________________

☐ **INTERGENERATIONAL FINANCIAL TRAUMA – Inherited wounds**

- Parents' or grandparents' financial trauma passed down through silence, fear, or scripts
- Immigrant family's economic struggles and survival mentality
- Family history of bankruptcy, depression-era scarcity

- Cultural or historical trauma affecting economic opportunity
- Other: ______________________________

Describe the inheritance: ______________________________

____

☐ COMPLEX FINANCIAL TRAUMA – Woven with other wounds

- Financial abuse in a relationship
- Money used as a tool of control or punishment in childhood
- Tying financial success to parental approval/love
- Financial stress during other trauma (illness, death, disaster)
- Other: ______________________________

Describe the complexity: ______________________________

Part B: The Cost of Silence

Have you ever spoken about these financial wounds before? ☐ Yes ☐ No ☐ Partially

If not, what has kept you silent? ______________________________________

What do you fear might happen if you spoke about it? ______________________________________

What might be possible if you broke the silence? ______________________________________

EXERCISE 6.5: HEALING REFLECTION – FROM WOUND TO WISDOM

Releasing What Was Never Yours to Carry

Part A: Belief Forensics

Take one painful financial experience from your timeline and examine the beliefs formed.

Experience: ______________________________

What I believed about money because of this: ______________________________

What I believed about myself because of this: ______________________________

What I believed about God/the world because of this: ______________________________

Evidence that these beliefs were protective at the time: ____

Evidence that these beliefs may no longer be true or helpful: ____

A truer, more compassionate belief I can now hold: ____

Part B: Compassionate Inquiry – Letter to Your Younger Self

Write a letter to yourself at the age when this wound was formed.

Dear [age] year-old me,

What you needed then, and didn't have,

was: ______________________________

What I want you to know now

is: ______________________________

You are not _______________________________ (the label you gave yourself).

You are

____

With love,

Your [current age] year-old self

Part C: The Compassionate Witness Exercise

Read your letter aloud to yourself, or to a trusted, non-judgmental listener.

How did it feel to write this letter? ____

How did it feel to read it? ____

What shifted, even slightly? ______________________________

____

____

EXERCISE 6.6: HEALING PRACTICE – FORGIVENESS AND RELEASE

Letting Go of What Weights You Down

____

Part A: What Needs to Be Forgiven?

Forgiveness is not condoning, forgetting, or excusing. It is releasing the burden of resentment so you can move forward.

I need to forgive:

☐ **Myself** for:

____

☐ **My parents/caregivers** for:

____

☐ **Others** (spouse, ex-spouse, family member, employer, advisor) for: ____

☐ **God / life / the universe** for:

____

☐ **Circumstances** (the system, the economy, bad luck) for:

____

____

Part B: The Release Statement

Write a statement of release. This is not about how the other person "deserves" forgiveness. It is about you no longer carrying this weight.

For myself:

"I forgive myself for

____

I did the best I could with what I knew and had at the time.

I release the shame and self-blame I have been carrying.

I am learning, and I am free to make different choices now."

For others:

"I release ______________________________ from the debt of

____

____.

Holding this against them has cost me

____

I am choosing to put down this weight, not because what happened was okay, but because I want to be free.

I entrust this to God/justice/time, and I move forward."

Part C: Ritual of Release

Consider a symbolic act of release. This can be private and simple.

Possible rituals:

☐ Write what you're releasing on paper, then burn it or tear it up

☐ Speak the release aloud in a place that feels significant

☐ Release something physically (a stone into water, a balloon into the sky)

☐ Pray or meditate, visualizing the weight lifting from your shoulders

☐ Share your release statement with a trusted witness

My release ritual: ______________________________________

____

Date of ritual: ______________________________________

How I felt afterward: ______________________________________

____

____

EXERCISE 6.7: REPAIRING YOUR RELATIONSHIP WITH MONEY

From Adversary to Tool

Part A: Money Metaphors

Complete this sentence without overthinking.

Money, to me, has been like a... ______________________________

(Example: a dangerous dog, a unreliable friend, a necessary evil, a rescuer, a scorecard)

Where did this metaphor come from? ____________________

How has this metaphor shaped your behavior? ________________

A new metaphor I want to try on: ______________________________

(Example: a tool, a river, a garden, a faithful servant, fuel)

What would change if you related to money this way? ______________________________

Part B: Rebuilding Trust – Small, Safe Experiments

When trust has been broken, it is rebuilt through small, consistent, positive experiences.

My financial trust has been broken by: ____

To rebuild trust with myself around money, I will start with these small, safe experiments:

Experiment	What I Will Do	Success Looks Like
1.		
2.		
3.		

Example experiments:

- Open my banking app for 30 seconds daily, without judgment
- Save $1 every day for one week
- Pay one bill as soon as it arrives, not when it's due
- Spend $5 on myself with explicit permission and no guilt

Part C: Reclaiming Agency

One financial decision I have been avoiding that I will take one small step toward this week:

The smallest possible next step is: ______________________________________

I will take this step on: ____________________________

Support I need: ____________________________________

EXERCISE 6.8: POST-TRAUMATIC FINANCIAL GROWTH

What Trauma Has Taught You

Part A: The Gift in the Wound

This is not to minimize pain. It is to recognize that you are not only wounded—you are also wiser.

What has your financial journey taught you about:

Your own strength? ____

What truly matters? ____

What you are capable of surviving? ____

____

How to discern who to trust? ____

____

The value of community/relationships? ______________________________

_

____

What you will never tolerate again? ____

____

What you want for others? ____

Part B: From Victim to Survivor to Steward

Where are you on this continuum?

☐ **Victim** – "This happened to me. I am powerless over money."
☐ **Survivor** – "I endured this. I am still here. I am learning."
☐ **Steward** – "I have been entrusted with resources, even small ones. I can use them wisely and purposefully."

What would help you move toward stewardship? ____

Part C: Your Financial Healing Affirmations

Write 3-5 affirmations that reflect your healing journey.

Example:

- *"My past is not my destiny. I am not defined by what I survived."*
- *"I am learning a new way to relate to money—with awareness, not fear."*
- *"I deserve financial peace. I am worthy of security."*
- *"Every small, wise choice is healing."*

1. ______________________________
2. ______________________________
3. ______________________________
4. ______________________________
5. ______________________________

BEHAVIORAL PRACTICE: 7-DAY FINANCIAL SELF-COMPASSION EXPERIMENT

Experiment Choice (choose one):

☐ **Experiment A: The Gentle Gaze** – Each day, open your primary financial account. Look at the balance for 30 seconds. Say to yourself: "*This is just data. It is not my worth.*"

☐ **Experiment B: Small Generosity to Self** – Each day, spend $1-2 on something that brings you genuine, guilt-free pleasure. Journal the experience.

☐ **Experiment C: Breaking the Silence** – Share one small piece of your financial story with a trusted, non-judgmental person.

☐ **Experiment D: The Compassion Journal** – Each evening, write one sentence of self-compassion about a financial struggle or fear you had that day.

Daily Log

Day	Experiment Activity	What I Noticed	Emotional Resistance (1-10)	What Shifted
1				
2				
3				
4				

Day	Experiment Activity	What I Noticed	Emotional Resistance (1-10)	What Shifted
5				
6				
7				

End-of-Week Reflection

What was the most difficult moment of this experiment? ______________________________

What was the most healing moment? ______________________________

What am I learning about being kind to myself around money? ____

____

One practice I will continue: ____

____

____

____

FAITH INTEGRATION

Healing and the Sacred

____

Scripture Meditation

"*He heals the brokenhearted and binds up their wounds.*" (Psalm 147:3)

"*The Lord is near to the brokenhearted and saves the crushed in spirit.*" (Psalm 34:18)

"*Behold, I am making all things new.*" (Revelation 21:5)

"*Come to me, all who labor and are heavy laden, and I will give you rest.*" (Matthew 11:28)

Part A: Bringing Your Financial Wounds to God

What financial pain have you never fully brought to God in prayer? ____

What keeps you from bringing it? ____

Write a prayer offering this wound to God:

Part B: God as Redeemer – Making All Things New

Is there any financial loss, mistake, or pain that you believe is beyond God's ability to redeem?

What would it mean to trust that God can bring good even from this? ______________________________

What might redemption of this situation look like? ______________________________

Part C: The Prodigal's Return – A Parable for You

Read Luke 15:11-24. The father ran to meet the son. There was no lecture, no shaming, no "I told you so." Just embrace and restoration.

What would it mean to believe that God runs toward you, not away from you, when it comes to your financial failures?

What would it mean to extend that same welcome to yourself? ______________________________

Part D: Prayer of Healing and Release

Pray this prayer aloud, slowly, or write your own.

"Lord,

I bring you my financial wounds—the ones I caused and the ones caused by others.
I bring you the shame I have carried, the fear that has driven me,
And the scarcity that has shrunk my heart and my vision.

I release the belief that my worth is measured by my wealth.
I release the need to punish myself for past mistakes.
I release the weight of inherited fears that were never mine to carry.

Heal my relationship with money.
Heal my relationship with myself.
Heal my relationship with You.

Make me a steward, not a slave.
Make me generous, not grasping.
Make me grateful, not grasping.

I receive Your healing now.

I receive Your welcome now.

I receive Your abundance now.

Amen."

CHAPTER 6 ACTION PLAN

One financial wound I will no longer allow to define me:

One scarcity belief I will actively challenge this month:

One self-compassion practice I will integrate into my financial routine:

One safe, healing experiment I will conduct:

One person I will share my financial healing journey with (therapist, trusted friend, clergy, support group):

One truth to remember:

"*He heals the brokenhearted and binds up their wounds.*" (Psalm 147:3)

CHAPTER 6 COMPLETION CHECKLIST

☐ I have completed my Financial Pain Timeline

☐ I have identified my earliest financial memory and its impact

☐ I have inventoried scarcity beliefs and survival behaviors

☐ I have mapped my personal scarcity loop

☐ I have written a letter to my younger self

☐ I have completed a forgiveness/release statement

☐ I have considered my financial metaphors and chosen a new one

☐ I have identified post-traumatic financial growth

☐ I have completed the 7-day behavioral experiment

☐ I have engaged with the faith integration reflection

☐ I am ready to proceed to Chapter 7

Date Completed: ____

My Key Insight from Chapter 6:

"Healing is not the erasure of the past. It is the integration of the past into a present that is no longer ruled by it. Your wounds become wisdom. Your scars become testimony. Your survival becomes strength. You are not what happened to you. You are what you have become in response."

CHAPTER 07

Social Influence and Money Behavior

Reclaiming Your Financial Autonomy

Learning Objectives

☐ Recognize how peer pressure and social comparison shape spending and saving habits
☐ Identify cultural and family norms that have become unconscious financial scripts
☐ Audit personal spending to uncover "social conformity" expenses
☐ Clarify personal financial values distinct from inherited or imposed values
☐ Develop boundary-setting skills for social financial situations
☐ Build an autonomous financial identity grounded in chosen values

---

Key Concepts Review

Term	Definition	In My Own Words
Social Comparison Theory	The drive to evaluate ourselves by comparing to others; can be upward (to those better off) or downward (to those worse off)	
Conspicuous Consumption	Spending on goods and services to publicly display economic power rather than to satisfy genuine needs	
Reference Group	The social group against which an individual evaluates their own status, behavior, and financial success	
Normative Social Influence	Conformity driven by the desire to be liked,	

Term	Definition	In My Own Words
	accepted, and belong to a group	
Informational Social Influence	Conformity driven by the assumption that others have accurate knowledge and we should follow their lead	
Lifestyle Creep	The gradual increase in discretionary spending as income rises, often driven by social comparison rather than genuine needs or values	
Financial Autonomy	The capacity to make financial decisions based on one's own values and goals, independent of social pressure	

Term	Definition	In My Own Words
Stealth Wealth	The practice of living below one's means and choosing not to display wealth through conspicuous consumption	
Values-Based Spending	Deliberately allocating financial resources in alignment with personally chosen core values	

EXERCISE 7.1: SOCIAL SPENDING AUDIT

Where Do You Spend to Fit In?

Part A: The Social Expense Inventory

Review your spending over the past 30-90 days. Identify purchases influenced by social factors.

Purchase	Amount	Social Context	Who Was I Trying to Be/Impress?	What Was I Trying to Signal?
Example: Expensive dinner with friends	$180	Colleague gathering	Successful, generous, "one of them"	I belong at this level
1.				
2.				
3.				
4.				
5.				
6.				

Purchase	Amount	Social Context	Who Was I Trying to Be/Impress?	What Was I Trying to Signal?

7.

Estimated total spent on social conformity in this period: $___________

Annualized estimate: $___________

What would this money have become in 10 years at 7% return? $___________ *(Estimate: annual × (1.07^10 - 1)/0.07)*

Part B: Social Pressure by Domain

Rate how much social pressure you feel in each area (1 = none, 5 = intense).

Domain	Pressure to Spend/Display	Source of Pressure (Peers, Family, Media, etc.)
Housing (size, location, style)	1 2 3 4 5	
Vehicle	1 2 3 4 5	
Clothing/Accessories	1 2 3 4 5	
Dining/Entertainment	1 2 3 4 5	
Travel/Vacations	1 2 3 4 5	
Gifts/Celebrations	1 2 3 4 5	
Children's activities/education	1 2 3 4 5	
Technology/Gadgets	1 2 3 4 5	

Domain	Pressure to Spend/Display	Source of Pressure (Peers, Family, Media, etc.)
Hobbies/Recreation	1 2 3 4 5	
Philanthropy/Giving	1 2 3 4 5	

Top three pressure domains:

1. ______
2. ______
3. ______

What would change if you released yourself from expectations in these areas?

______

______

______

Part C: The Motivation Audit

For your top three social expenses from Part A, dig deeper.

Expense 1: ____

On a scale of 1-10, how much of this purchase was for:

Motivation	Rating (1-10)
My genuine enjoyment/utility	
To avoid judgment or awkwardness	
To gain approval or admiration	
To feel equal to peers	
To feel superior or ahead	
To maintain a relationship	

What need was I really trying to meet?
☐ Belonging ☐ Validation ☐ Status ☐ Love ☐ Security ☐ Other: ____________________________

A non-spending way to meet this need: ____________________________

Expense 2: ____

On a scale of 1-10, how much of this purchase was for:

Motivation	Rating (1-10)
My genuine enjoyment/utility	
To avoid judgment or awkwardness	
To gain approval or admiration	
To feel equal to peers	
To feel superior or ahead	
To maintain a relationship	

What need was I really trying to meet?
☐ Belonging ☐ Validation ☐ Status ☐ Love ☐ Security ☐ Other: ___________________________

A non-spending way to meet this need: ___________________________

Expense 3: ____

What need was I really trying to meet?
☐ Belonging ☐ Validation ☐ Status ☐ Love ☐ Security ☐ Other: ________________________

A non-spending way to meet this need: ________________________

EXERCISE 7.2: CULTURAL MONEY NORMS INVENTORY

Whose Scripts Are You Following?

Part A: Inherited Financial Messages

Complete this inventory across the different "cultures" you inhabit.

Source	Explicit Messages ("They said...")	Implicit Messages ("They showed/modeled ...")	Emotional Tone
Family of Origin			
Religious/Spiritual Community			
Ethnic/Cultural Heritage			
Professional/Workplace Culture			
Peer Group/Friends			
Geographic Region			

Part B: The Conformity Cost – Personal Examples

A time I spent money to conform to family expectations: ____________________

What did it cost me financially? ____________________

What did it cost me emotionally/psychologically? ____________________

A time I spent money to conform to professional/peer expectations: ____________________

What did it cost me financially? ____________________

What did it cost me emotionally/psychologically? ____________________

A time I did NOT spend money to conform, and faced social consequences: ______________________________

____

What happened? ______________________________

_

How did I handle it? ______________________________

What did I learn? ______________________________

____

____

Part C: The "Should" Deconstruction

Complete these sentences from your various cultural scripts.

According to my family, I should: ______________________________

____

According to my culture/ethnic community, I should: ______________________________

According to my profession/industry, I should: ______________________________

According to my friends/peers, I should: ______________________________

According to social media/media, I should: ______________________________

Now, circle the "shoulds" that actually align with who you want to be.

Cross out the ones you want to release.

EXERCISE 7.3: THE KEEPING UP WITH THE JONESES DIAGNOSTIC

Who Are Your Joneses?

Part A: Identify Your Reference Groups

List the people or groups you unconsciously compare yourself to financially.

Reference Person/Group	Relationship	Domain of Comparison	Emotional Effect	Behavioral Effect
Example: College roommate	Former peer	Career success, home ownership	Envy, inadequacy	Urge to upgrade home
1.				
2.				

Reference Person/Group	Relationship	Domain of Comparison	Emotional Effect	Behavioral Effect
3.				
4.				
5.				

Part B: The Joneses Scorecard

Rate how much you agree with each statement (1 = Strongly Disagree, 5 = Strongly Agree).

Statement	1	2	3	4	5
I frequently compare my financial situation to others my age.	☐	☐	☐	☐	☐

Statement	1	2	3	4	5
Social media often makes me feel like I'm falling behind.	☐	☐	☐	☐	☐
I've made purchases I couldn't afford to avoid looking cheap.	☐	☐	☐	☐	☐
I feel pressure to keep up with my neighbors/colleagues.	☐	☐	☐	☐	☐
I worry that people will judge me based on what I drive/wear/own.	☐	☐	☐	☐	☐
I feel anxious when friends discuss expensive purchases or vacations.	☐	☐	☐	☐	☐
I've hidden financial sacrifices to appear more successful.	☐	☐	☐	☐	☐

Statement	1	2	3	4	5
My spending goals are often influenced by what others have.	☐	☐	☐	☐	☐

Total Score: ____ /40

Interpretation:

- **8-16:** Low social comparison tendency
- **17-24:** Moderate social comparison tendency
- **25-32:** High social comparison tendency
- **33-40:** Very high; comparison may be significantly driving financial behavior

Reflection: Does this score surprise you? Why or why not?

___

Part C: The Cost of Keeping Up

What has "keeping up with the Joneses" cost you?

Type of Cost	Specific Examples	Estimated Amount/Impact
Financial (debt, missed savings, lost investment growth)		$
Emotional (anxiety, envy, shame, inadequacy)		
Relational (competition, secrecy, resentment)		
Time (hours spent working to afford, shopping, comparing)		
Identity (loss of authentic self, values compromise)		

What is the single greatest cost you have paid? ______________________________

____

EXERCISE 7.4: VALUES CLARIFICATION

What Do You Actually Believe?

Part A: Values Card Sort – Identifying Your Top 5

Below is a list of common values. Circle the 10 that resonate most deeply with you. Then, rank your top 5.

Adventure	Authority	Autonomy	Beauty	Caring
Challenge	Community	Compassion	Competence	Connection
Contribution	Courage	Creativity	Dignity	Discipline
Education	Equality	Excellence	Faith	Family
Freedom	Friendship	Fulfillment	Generosity	Gratitude
Growth	Health	Honesty	Honor	Hope

Humility	Independence	Integrity	Intimacy	Joy
Justice	Kindness	Knowledge	Leisure	Love
Loyalty	Meaning	Moderation	Nature	Openness
Order	Passion	Peace	Pleasure	Purpose
Recognition	Reliability	Resilience	Respect	Responsibility
Security	Service	Simplicity	Spirituality	Stability
Strength	Success	Tradition	Tranquility	Trust
Truth	Vitality	Wealth	Wisdom	Wonder

My Top 10 Values (in no order):

1. ________________ 6. ________________
2. ________________ 7. ________________
3. ________________ 8. ________________
4. ________________ 9. ________________
5. ________________ 10. ________________

Now, narrow to your Top 5:

1. ______________________________________

2. ______________________________________

3. ______________________________________

4. ______________________________________

5. ______________________________________

Part B: Values Definition – What Do These Mean to You?

For each of your Top 5 values, write what it means in your own words.

Value 1: ______________________________________

This means to me: ______________________________________

Value 2: ______________________________________

This means to me: ______________________________________

Value 3: ____

This means to me: ____

____

Value 4: ____

This means to me: ____

____

Value 5: ____

This means to me: ____

____

____

Part C: Values-Expenditure Gap Analysis

For each of your Top 5 values, assess how well your current spending aligns.

Value	Current Spending Alignment (1-10)	Evidence of Alignment	Evidence of Gap	One Change to Increase Alignment
1.				
2.				
3.				
4.				
5.				

What does this gap analysis reveal? ____

____

Where is the largest gap between what you say you value and how you spend? ______________________________

____

EXERCISE 7.5: THE AUTONOMY AUDIT

Whose Life Are You Living?

Part A: The Mirror Test

Answer these questions as honestly as you can.

If no one were watching, judging, or comparing, how would my financial life be different?

What would I spend less on? ____

What would I spend more on? ____

What would I save for? ______________________________

What would I stop feeling guilty about? ______________________________

What would I stop feeling proud of? ______________________________

What would I do with my time that I don't do now? ______________________________

Part B: The Legacy Question

Imagine your 80-year-old self, looking back on your financial life.

What financial decisions would that older version of you be proud of? ______________________________

____

____

What financial decisions would that older version of you regret? ______________________________

____

____

What would that older self tell you about the importance of others' opinions? ______________________________

____

____

____

Part C: Your Financial Autonomy Statement

Write a personal declaration of financial independence from social comparison.

"I, ____________________, hereby declare that my financial life belongs to me.

I release myself from the need to: ____

____

I give myself permission to: ____

____

I measure financial success by: ____

____

I will not apologize for: ____

____

I will not boast about: ____

____

My money serves my values, not my image.

Signed: ______________________________ Date: _______________

EXERCISE 7.6: BOUNDARY PRACTICE – THE ART OF SAYING NO

Protecting Your Financial Sovereignty

Part A: Common Social Financial Pressures

Check situations where you feel pressure to spend.

Situation	☐ Feel Pressure	Typical Response	Desired Response
Expensive group dinner/event	☐		
Destination wedding/bachelorette	☐		

Situation	☐ Feel Pressure	Typical Response	Desired Response
Expensive gift exchange	☐		
Colleagues going out after work	☐		
Friends planning costly vacation	☐		
Pressure to donate to cause/event	☐		
Keeping up with neighborhood/home standards	☐		
Children's activities/parties	☐		

Situation	☐ Feel Pressure	Typical Response	Desired Response
Luxury brand expectations	☐		
Tipping pressure	☐		
Other: ______________	☐		

Part B: Scripting Your Boundaries

For each situation, prepare a response that is gracious, firm, and values-aligned.

Situation 1: ____

My boundary: ____

Script: "____ "

Situation 2: ______________________________

My boundary: ______________________________

Script: "______________________________"

Situation 3: ______________________________

My boundary: ______________________________

Script: "______________________________"

Sample scripts for reference:

- *"That sounds lovely, but it's not in my budget right now. I'd love to celebrate with you another way."*
- *"I'm focusing on some financial goals this year, so I'll have to pass. Please save me the details though!"*
- *"I'd rather host a potluck at my place so we can all spend time together without the expense."*

- *"I don't give gifts for that occasion, but I'd be happy to contribute in another way."*
- *"I'm working on simplifying my life, and that includes being more intentional about what I buy."*

Part C: The Boundary Experiment

This week, I will say "no" to one unnecessary social expense.

The situation: ____

My script: ____

Date/Time: ____

How did it feel to set the boundary? ____

What was the outcome? ____

What did I learn? ____

EXERCISE 7.7: BUILDING YOUR FINANCIAL TRIBE

Finding Your People

Part A: Current Social Ecosystem

Map your current financial social influences.

Person/Group	Do They Support or Pressure My Financial Autonomy?	Do We Share Similar Financial Values?	Do I Feel Safe Discussing Money Here?

Part B: Desired Financial Community

What would a "financial tribe" that supports your autonomy look like? ____________________________

What values would they share? ____________________________

What conversations would you have? ____________________________

Where might you find such people? ____________________________

☐ Financial independence/local FIRE group
☐ Values-based investing community
☐ Faith-based stewardship group
☐ Minimalist/simple living community
☐ Book club focused on money/philosophy
☐ Online forum/community (specify: _______________)
☐ Create my own with like-minded friends

☐ Other:

____

Part C: One Connection This Month

One person I will reach out to for a values-based money conversation: ______________________________

What I will say: ____

Date by which I will do this: ______________________

EXERCISE 7.8: STEALTH WEALTH – THE QUIET REBELLION

Finding Freedom in Invisibility

Part A: What Does "Stealth Wealth" Mean to You?

Stealth wealth is not deprivation; it is the intentional choice to allocate resources to private meaning rather than public display.

What appeals to you about this concept? ______________________________

____

What feels challenging or uncomfortable? ______________________________

____

____

Part B: Stealth Wealth Planning

Identify areas where you can shift from conspicuous to inconspicuous consumption.

Area	Current (Conspicuous)	Desired (Inconspicuous)	Private Joy I Will Gain
Vehicle			
Home			

Area	Current (Conspicuous)	Desired (Inconspicuous)	Private Joy I Will Gain
Clothing			
Dining/Entertainment			
Travel			
Hobbies			
Gifts			
Technology			

Part C: My Stealth Wealth Commitment

I commit to one stealth wealth practice this month:

The private satisfaction I expect from this: ____

After one month, reflect:

What did I learn? ____

How did it feel to not display this? ____

Would I continue? ☐ Yes ☐ No ☐ Modified

BEHAVIORAL PRACTICE: 7-DAY SOCIAL INFLUENCE AWARENESS EXPERIMENT

Experiment Choice (choose one):

☐ **Experiment A: The Comparison Fast** – For 7 days, consciously avoid all financial comparison. Unfollow triggers. When comparison thoughts arise, gently redirect. Journal daily.

☐ **Experiment B: The "No" Practice** – Deliberately decline ONE social spending invitation. Use your script. Journal the experience.

☐ **Experiment C: The Values-Based Purchase** – Make ONE purchase this week that is purely aligned with your values, not at all influenced by social pressure. Journal the experience.

☐ **Experiment D: The Stealth Wealth Day** – For one full day, make all financial choices invisible. No logos, no brand signaling, no mentioning costs. Observe your internal experience.

Daily Log

Day	Experiment Activity	Social Pressure Encountered?	Response	What I Noticed About Myself
1				
2				

Day	Experiment Activity	Social Pressure Encountered?	Response	What I Noticed About Myself
3				
4				
5				
6				
7				

End-of-Week Reflection

What was the most difficult moment of this experiment? ________________________________

What was the most freeing moment? ________________________________

____

What did I learn about my need for social approval around money? ________________________________

____

What did I learn about my capacity for financial autonomy? ________________________________

____

One practice I will continue: ________________________________

____

____

FAITH INTEGRATION

Non-Conformity and Transformation

Scripture Meditation

"*Do not be conformed to this world, but be transformed by the renewal of your mind, that by testing you may discern what is the will of God, what is good and acceptable and perfect.*" (Romans 12:2)

"*I have learned in whatever situation I am to be content. I know how to be brought low, and I know how to abound. In any and every circumstance, I have learned the secret of facing plenty and hunger, abundance and need.*" (Philippians 4:11-12)

"*You adulterous people! Do you not know that friendship with the world is enmity with God?*" (James 4:4)

"*For what does it profit a man to gain the whole world and forfeit his soul?*" (Mark 8:36)

Part A: Conformity and the Spiritual Life

In what ways has the "world" (cultural values) shaped my financial priorities? ______________________________

____

____

Where do I feel the tension between cultural definitions of success and spiritual definitions of faithfulness?

____

____

What would "non-conformity" look like in my financial life? ______________________________

____

____

____

Part B: Contentment as Spiritual Discipline

On a scale of 1-10, how content am I with my current financial circumstances?

1 ☐ 2 ☐ 3 ☐ 4 ☐ 5 ☐ 6 ☐ 7 ☐ 8 ☐ 9 ☐ 10 ☐

What stands between me and greater contentment? ______________________________

____

What is the difference between contentment and complacency? ______________________________

____

Paul said he "learned the secret" of contentment. What might I need to learn?

____

____

____

Part C: Prayer for Discernment

Write a prayer asking for the wisdom to distinguish cultural pressure from divine calling.

____

____

Part D: Faith-Based Financial Autonomy Statement

Complete this statement from your faith perspective.

Because I belong to God and not to the world, I am free to:

Because my worth is determined by my Creator and not my consumption, I release:

Because I am a steward, not an owner, I will:

CHAPTER 7 ACTION PLAN

One social pressure I will consciously resist this month:

One boundary I will set or strengthen:

One comparison trigger I will eliminate or reduce:

One values-aligned purchase or saving choice I will make:

One person/community I will connect with for financial encouragement:

One truth to remember:

"Do not be conformed to this world, but be transformed by the renewal of your mind." (Romans 12:2)

CHAPTER 7 COMPLETION CHECKLIST

☐ I have completed the Social Spending Audit
☐ I have inventoried cultural money norms and their sources
☐ I have identified my "Joneses" and calculated the cost of comparison
☐ I have clarified my Top 5 personal values
☐ I have conducted a Values-Expenditure Gap Analysis
☐ I have written my Financial Autonomy Statement
☐ I have scripted at least one boundary-setting response
☐ I have completed the boundary experiment (saying "no")
☐ I have considered my "stealth wealth" opportunities
☐ I have completed the 7-day behavioral experiment
☐ I have engaged with the faith integration reflection
☐ I am ready to proceed to Chapter 8

Date Completed: ___________________________________

My Key Insight from Chapter 7:

"The greatest financial independence is not just independence from debt or a boss, but independence from the need for external validation through consumption. It is the quiet, unshakeable confidence that your worth is not a number in a bank account, but the sum of your character, your connections, and the purposeful life you are building—on your own terms."

CHAPTER 08

Purpose, Meaning, and Stewardship

Aligning Your Finances with Your Calling

Learning Objectives

☐ Connect money to a deeper sense of purpose and vocation
☐ Understand stewardship as a theological and practical framework
☐ Develop a comprehensive stewardship plan across income, saving, giving, and spending
☐ Align financial decisions with personal calling and values
☐ Move from ownership to trusteeship in relationship with money
☐ Cultivate generosity as a spiritual discipline and source of joy

Key Concepts Review

Term	Definition	In My Own Words
Stewardship	The management of resources entrusted to one's care, recognizing that ultimate ownership belongs to God or a higher purpose	
Calling/Vocation	The unique purpose or work to which an individual is divinely or existentially summoned; the intersection of gifts, passions, and the world's needs	
Eudaimonia	Aristotelian concept of human flourishing through the active exercise of virtue and the realization of one's potential	

Term	Definition	In My Own Words
Generativity	Erik Erikson's concept of concern for establishing and guiding the next generation; a hallmark of psychological maturity	
Prosocial Spending	Using money to benefit others, which research shows reliably increases well-being more than spending on oneself	
Warm Glow Effect	The intrinsic emotional reward experienced when giving to others; a measurable neurological and psychological phenomenon	
Legacy	The financial, relational, and values-based inheritance	

Term	Definition	In My Own Words
	one leaves for future generations	
Purpose Alignment	The degree to which financial decisions reflect and advance one's core life purpose	

EXERCISE 8.1: PURPOSE MAPPING

Discovering What Your Money Is For

Part A: Your Calling – Beyond What You Do

Before connecting money to purpose, we must clarify purpose itself.

When have I felt most alive, most myself, most "in flow"?

What problems in the world break my heart? ___

What am I uniquely positioned to do or offer – by virtue of my gifts, experiences, relationships, and resources?

If I knew I could not fail, what would I attempt? ___

What do I want my life to have meant? ___

My calling (in one sentence) is:

Part B: Money and Purpose – The Connection

How does money serve your calling? Answer honestly, not ideally.

My Calling/Purpose	How Money Currently Serves This Purpose	How Money Could Better Serve This Purpose

Example:

My Calling	Current Role of Money	Desired Role of Money
Mentoring young people in my field	I earn income from my work, which funds my life	I could create a scholarship fund, offer pro-bono mentoring time, reduce work hours to volunteer

---

Part C: The Purpose Alignment Gap

On a scale of 1-10, how aligned are your current financial decisions with your sense of calling?

1 ☐ 2 ☐ 3 ☐ 4 ☐ 5 ☐ 6 ☐ 7 ☐ 8 ☐ 9 ☐ 10 ☐
(1 = "Completely misaligned," 10 = "Perfectly aligned")

What contributes to the gap? ____

What would closing the gap by just 1 point look like? ____

What is one financial decision you could make this month that would increase alignment?

Part D: The Purpose Budget – A Vision Exercise

Imagine you had perfect financial freedom. Not unlimited wealth, but enough. Answer in present tense.

I allocate my time to: ____________________

I allocate my money to: ____________________

I allocate my attention to: ____________________

I am able to say "yes" to: ____________________

I am able to say "no" to: ______________________________________

The people I serve are: ______________________________________

The impact I see is: ______________________________________

What is the smallest step toward this vision that I can take this week? ______________________________________

EXERCISE 8.2: STEWARDSHIP THEOLOGY AND PHILOSOPHY

From Owner to Trustee

Part A: Your Stewardship Heritage

What messages about ownership and stewardship did you receive growing up?

Source	Message (Explicit or Implicit)
Family	
Faith community	
Culture	
Personal experience	

Who modeled faithful stewardship for you? ______________________________

What did they do that you admired? ____

____

____

Part B: The Ownership Illusion

Stewardship begins with the recognition that we are not ultimate owners.

What do I "own" that, in truth, was given to me?

☐ My life/body ☐ My talents/abilities ☐ My education ☐ My family ☐ My faith ☐ My financial resources ☐ Other: _____

How might my relationship with money change if I truly believed it was not "mine" but entrusted to me?

____

____

What would I do differently? ____

____

What would I stop doing? ____

____

____

Part C: A Stewardship Prayer or Affirmation

Write a personal stewardship statement or prayer.

"I acknowledge that everything I have is a gift, not an entitlement.

I am not an owner; I am a trustee.

I hold these resources for a time, and I will be accountable for how I use them.

Therefore, I commit to: ____

____

I release the need to: ____

____

I ask for wisdom to manage well, courage to give generously, and joy in the stewardship itself.

Amen."

EXERCISE 8.3: THE STEWARDSHIP PLAN

A Framework for Faithful Allocation

Part A: The Four Stewardship Buckets

A comprehensive stewardship plan allocates resources across four domains.

Bucket	Purpose	Current %	Target %	Current $	Target $
1. INCOME	The river, not the reservoir. How you generate resources.	100 %	100 %		

Bucket	Purpose	Current %	Target %	Current $	Target $
2. GIVING	Resources returned to God/community/purpose				
3. SAVING	Resources stored for future needs and opportunities				
4. INVESTING	Resources deployed for growth and impact				
5. SPENDING	Resources used for daily living and flourishing				

Note: Giving, Saving, Investing, and Spending are percentages of your Income. They should add to 100%.

Part B: Income – The River

My current primary sources of income:

1. ______
2. ______
3. ______

Does my work align with my sense of calling? ☐ Yes ☐ Partially ☐ No

If not, what is one step toward greater alignment? ______

Is my income sufficient for faithful stewardship of my responsibilities?

☐ Yes ☐ No – I need to increase earning capacity ☐ No – I need to reduce obligations

One action to strengthen my income river: ______

Part C: Giving – The First Fruit

Stewardship traditions often prioritize giving as the first allocation, not what's left over.

My current giving practice:

☐ I give spontaneously, without a plan
☐ I give a percentage of my income
☐ I give a fixed dollar amount
☐ I do not currently give
☐ Other:

____

Current giving rate: ***% of income OR $__*** per month/year

Desired giving rate: ***% of income OR $__*** per month/year

My Giving Vision:

Causes/organizations I am passionate about: ____

The impact I want my giving to have: ____

How I want to involve my family in giving: ______________________

____

One change I will make to my giving practice this year: ______________________

____

____

Generosity Experiment:

This month, I will give something away – money, time, or resources – and journal the experience.

What I gave: ______________________

To whom/where: ______________________

How I felt during the act: ______________________

How I felt afterward: ______________________

What I learned: ______________________

Part D: Saving – The Buffer

Stewardship requires prudence; saving is not hoarding but preparing.

My current emergency fund: ____ months of essential expenses

Target: ____ months (recommended: 3-6 months)

My other savings goals:

Goal	Target Amount	Target Date	Current Progress
	$		$
	$		$
	$		$
	$		$

One action to strengthen my savings buffer: ____

Part E: Investing – Deployed Resources

Stewards invest to preserve purchasing power, generate resources for future purposes, and sometimes to create impact.

My current investment approach: ___________________________

My investment philosophy (circle):
☐ Maximize return ☐ Balance risk/return ☐ Values-aligned/ESG ☐ Impact-first ☐ Unsure

Do my investments align with my values and purpose? ☐ Yes ☐ Partially ☐ No ☐ I don't know

If no or partially, what is one change I could make? ___________________________

My desired investment allocation:

Asset Class	Current %	Target %
Cash/Savings		
Bonds/Fixed Income		
Stocks/Equities		
Real Estate		
Other		
TOTAL	**100%**	**100%**

Part F: Spending – Daily Stewardship

How we spend the small amounts reveals our true priorities.

My spending currently reflects these priorities: ______________________________

My spending should reflect these priorities: ____________________________________

The largest gap between current and desired spending: ____________________________________

One spending change I will make this month: ____________________________________

EXERCISE 8.4: THE GENEROSITY INVENTORY

Beyond Money – The Fullness of Stewardship

Part A: Beyond Financial Giving

Stewardship is not only about money. Inventory the full range of your resources.

Resource	How I Currently Share This	How I Could Share More
Time		
Talent/Skills		
Attention		
Hospitality (space, home, table)		
Wisdom/Experience		
Encouragement		
Network/Connections		
Emotional presence		

Part B: The Reciprocity of Generosity

Research shows that giving benefits the giver as much as the receiver.

What have I received from being generous? ______________________________

____

What do I fear about becoming more generous? ______________________________

____

What belief about scarcity holds me back from generosity? ______________________________

____

What would it take to release that belief? ______________________________

____

____

EXERCISE 8.5: LEGACY AND GENERATIVITY

What Will Outlive You?

Part A: Defining Your Legacy

Legacy is not only for the wealthy or the elderly. You are building it now.

What do I want to leave behind – financially and non-financially?

Domain	What I Want to Leave	To Whom/For What Purpose
Financial assets		
Values/Beliefs		
Stories/Wisdom		

Domain	What I Want to Leave	To Whom/For What Purpose
Skills/Knowledge		
Reputation/Character		
Relationships		
Impact on community/world		

Part B: The Legacy Letter – Draft

Write a draft of a letter to be read by your heirs or community after your life.

"To those I leave behind,

What I want you to know about the money I leave you is: ______________________________

What I want you to know about the life I lived is: ______________________________

____

What I hope you will do with what I've left is: ______________________________

____

What I hope you will become is: ______________________________

____

I am grateful for: ______________________________

____

I am sorry for: ______________________________

____

With love,

____

Part C: Generativity – Investing in the Next Generation

Generativity is the concern for and commitment to the next generation.

How am I currently investing in those who will come after me?

☐ Mentoring/teaching
☐ Parenting/grandparenting
☐ Creating institutions or organizations
☐ Environmental stewardship
☐ Passing on skills or trades
☐ Sharing wisdom/stories
☐ Financial provision
☐ Other:

____

One new generative practice I will begin: __________________________________

EXERCISE 8.6: STEWARDSHIP IN DAILY LIFE – RITUALS AND PRACTICES

Weaving Purpose into Routine

Part A: Stewardship Rituals

Small, repeated practices shape our identity as stewards.

Rituals I already have that connect me to purpose: ______________________________

Rituals I want to develop:

Ritual	When/How Often	Purpose
Example: Pre-payday prayer	Before each paycheck	Acknowledge God as source
1.		
2.		
3.		

Ideas for stewardship rituals:

- Pray over your paycheck before depositing it
- Light a candle when making financial decisions
- Keep a giving journal, noting where your money went and how it felt
- Share a "stewardship story" at family meals
- Begin budget meetings with gratitude
- Write thank-you notes to those who have invested in you

Part B: The Weekly Stewardship Review

A structured practice for aligning your week with your purpose.

Each week, I will ask myself:

1. How did I use my resources this week in ways that aligned with my purpose?

2. Where did I miss an opportunity to be a faithful steward?

3. What is one thing I will do differently next week?

4. What am I grateful for in this season of stewardship?

EXERCISE 8.7: THE STEWARDSHIP AUDIT – ANNUAL REVIEW

Taking Account of What Has Been Entrusted

Part A: Annual Stewardship Reflection

Set aside time annually to complete this comprehensive review.

The Past Year:

How did I generate income? Was my work aligned with my calling?

How did I give? Was my giving intentional, joyful, and impactful?

How did I save? Did I build appropriate reserves for future needs?

How did I invest? Did I deploy resources wisely, for growth and good?

How did I spend? Did my daily expenditures reflect my values?

What financial mistakes did I make? What did I learn?

What financial decisions am I proud of? Why?

What was my overall "stewardship grade" for this year? A B C D F

Why?

Part B: The Year Ahead

My primary stewardship goal for next year is:

____

The greatest opportunity I see
is: ____

____

The greatest challenge I anticipate
is: ____

____

The support or resources I need
is: ____

____

One verse, quote, or principle I will carry into this
year: ______________________________________

____

____

BEHAVIORAL PRACTICE: 7-DAY STEWARDSHIP AWARENESS EXPERIMENT

Experiment Choice (choose one):

☐ **Experiment A: The Purpose Pause** – Before any non-trivial financial decision this week, pause and ask: "*Does this align with my purpose and values?*" Journal each instance.

☐ **Experiment B: Daily Generosity** – Each day, give something away – money, time, attention, encouragement. Notice how it affects your sense of abundance or scarcity.

☐ **Experiment C: The Stewardship Ritual** – Create and practice one daily stewardship ritual (e.g., gratitude before spending, prayer over paycheck). Journal the experience.

☐ **Experiment D: The Legacy Letter Draft** – Spend 15 minutes each day drafting your legacy letter. By week's end, have a complete first draft.

Daily Log

Day	Experiment Activity	What I Noticed	Emotional State	Insight About Purpose/Stewardship
1				
2				
3				
4				
5				
6				
7				

End-of-Week Reflection

What was the most meaningful moment of this experiment? ____

What did I learn about the connection between my money and my purpose? ______________________________

What resistance to stewardship did I encounter? ______________________________

What joy did I discover? ______________________________

_

One practice I will continue: ______________________________

FAITH INTEGRATION

Faithful Stewardship as Worship

Scripture Meditation

"*Moreover, it is required of stewards that they be found faithful.*" (1 Corinthians 4:2)

"*The earth is the Lord's and the fullness thereof, the world and those who dwell therein.*" (Psalm 24:1)

"*For where your treasure is, there your heart will be also.*" (Matthew 6:21)

"*Each one must give as he has decided in his heart, not reluctantly or under compulsion, for God loves a cheerful giver.*" (2 Corinthians 9:7)

"*You shall remember the Lord your God, for it is he who gives you power to get wealth.*" (Deuteronomy 8:18)

Part A: God as Owner, You as Steward

If I truly believed that God owns everything and I am merely a manager, what would change?

What would I stop worrying about? ______________________________

What would I start doing differently? ______________________________

What would I do with more courage? ______________________________

Part B: Faithfulness, Not Success

"It is required of stewards that they be found faithful" – not successful, not impressive, not wealthy. Faithful.

Where do I confuse financial success with spiritual faithfulness? ______________________________

Where do I need to release outcomes to God and focus on faithful actions? ______________________________

What would it look like to measure my financial life by faithfulness rather than returns?

Part C: A Prayer of Dedication

Write a prayer dedicating your financial life to God.

Part D: Stewardship as Spiritual Discipline

Stewardship is not a duty; it is a discipline that forms our character.

What is God teaching me through money right now? ______________________________

Where am I being invited to trust more? ______________________________

Where am I being invited to release more? ______________________________

Where am I being invited to risk more for the sake of the Kingdom? ______________________________

CHAPTER 8 ACTION PLAN

One purpose-aligned financial decision I will make this month:

One change to my giving practice I will implement:

One stewardship ritual I will begin:

One step toward the stewardship vision I wrote in Exercise 8.1:

One person I will share my legacy letter or stewardship vision with:

One truth to remember:

"It is required of stewards that they be found faithful." (1 Corinthians 4:2)

CHAPTER 8 COMPLETION CHECKLIST

☐ I have completed the Purpose Mapping exercise
☐ I have articulated my calling in one sentence
☐ I have assessed the alignment between my money and my purpose
☐ I have drafted a personal stewardship prayer/statement
☐ I have completed the Four Buckets Stewardship Plan
☐ I have set goals for giving, saving, investing, and spending
☐ I have completed the Generosity Inventory (beyond money)
☐ I have drafted a Legacy Letter
☐ I have designed at least one stewardship ritual
☐ I have completed the 7-day behavioral experiment
☐ I have engaged with the faith integration reflection
☐ I am ready to proceed to the Conclusion

Date Completed: ______________________________

My Key Insight from Chapter 8:

"The earth is the Lord's and everything in it. We are not owners; we are tenants. We are not masters; we are managers. We are not kings; we are stewards. And to be a faithful steward—to take what has been entrusted and use it for the purposes of the Owner—this is not a burden. It is a dignity. It is a calling. It is worship."

CHAPTER 09

Contentment, Gratitude, and Peace

Finding Enough in a Culture of More

Learning Objectives

☐ Understand contentment as a learnable skill, not a circumstantial outcome
☐ Cultivate gratitude as a counterbalance to the hedonic treadmill
☐ Identify the psychological and spiritual roots of financial

anxiety

☐ Develop practices to reduce money-related worry and increase peace

☐ Distinguish between the "enough" of contentment and the "never enough" of consumer culture

☐ Build a daily rhythm of gratitude and financial sabbath

Key Concepts Review

Term	Definition	In My Own Words
Contentment	A state of inner sufficiency and peace that is not dependent on external circumstances; a learnable skill, not a personality trait	
Hedonic Treadmill	The tendency to return to a stable happiness baseline after positive or negative events, requiring ever-greater	

Term	Definition	In My Own Words
	achievements to maintain satisfaction	
Aspiration Adaptation	The process by which expectations and desires rise in tandem with achievements, ensuring that "enough" remains perpetually out of reach	
Gratitude	The practice of recognizing and appreciating what one has received, both from others and from life; a powerful antidote to envy and dissatisfaction	
Enough	A psychological and spiritual threshold beyond which additional accumulation does not increase well-being; the recognition of sufficiency	

Term	Definition	In My Own Words
Financial Sabbath	A regular practice of rest from financial worry, spending, and consumption; a disciplined pause to remember what is not for sale	
Social Comparison	The drive to evaluate oneself in comparison to others; the primary engine of status anxiety and consumer dissatisfaction	
Scarcity Loop	The self-reinforcing cycle of perceived lack, anxiety, and compensatory behavior that perpetuates a sense of insufficiency	

EXERCISE 9.1: THE GRATITUDE LEDGER

Recognizing What Money Cannot Buy

Part A: The Non-Monetary Wealth Inventory

List 10 things that enrich your life that money cannot purchase.

Money cannot buy:

1. ____________________
2. ____________________
3. ____________________
4. ____________________
5. ____________________
6. ____________________
7. ____________________
8. ____________________
9. ____________________
10. ____________________

Reflection:

Which of these do I most take for granted? ______________________________

____

Which of these would I miss most if they were gone? ______________________________

____

What would it mean to treat these as forms of wealth? ______________________________

____

____

Part B: Daily Gratitude Practice – 7-Day Ledger

Each day, write 3 specific things you are grateful for that are unrelated to money or consumption.

Day	Gratitude 1	Gratitude 2	Gratitude 3
1			
2			
3			
4			
5			
6			
7			

Part C: The Gratitude Audit

Reflect on your financial life specifically.

I am grateful for these financial provisions (however small):

1. ______
2. ______
3. ______
4. ______
5. ______

I am grateful for these financial lessons (even the hard ones):

1. ______
2. ______
3. ______

I am grateful for these people who have helped me financially or taught me about money:

1. ______
2. ______
3. ______

Part D: Gratitude Letter – Financial Edition

Write a brief letter of gratitude to someone who has positively influenced your financial life. (You may choose to send it or not.)

Dear _______________,

I am writing to thank you for

____

Because of you, I have learned

____

I remember when

____

Your influence has shaped

____

With gratitude,

____

EXERCISE 9.2: THE CONTENTMENT DIAGNOSTIC

How Much Is Enough?

Part A: The Contentment Scale

Rate each statement honestly from 1 (Strongly Disagree) to 5 (Strongly Agree).

Statement	1	2	3	4	5
I frequently feel that I don't have enough.	☐	☐	☐	☐	☐
I can enjoy what I have without comparing to others.	☐	☐	☐	☐	☐

Statement	1	2	3	4	5
I believe that more money would solve most of my problems.	☐	☐	☐	☐	☐
I am able to be happy for others' financial success without envy.	☐	☐	☐	☐	☐
I often think, "If only I had [X], then I'd be satisfied."	☐	☐	☐	☐	☐
I feel at peace when I consider my financial situation.	☐	☐	☐	☐	☐
I worry that I'm falling behind where I "should" be.	☐	☐	☐	☐	☐
I regularly experience gratitude for what I have.	☐	☐	☐	☐	☐
I believe that contentment is something I can learn.	☐	☐	☐	☐	☐

Statement	1	2	3	4	5
I feel pressure to keep up with others my age.	☐	☐	☐	☐	☐

Scoring:

- **Contentment indicators:** Items 2, 4, 6, 8, 9 (higher scores = greater contentment)
- **Discontentment indicators:** Items 1, 3, 5, 7, 10 (lower scores = greater contentment)

My primary contentment challenges are: ______________________________

____

____

Part B: The "Enough" Threshold

Answer these questions as honestly as you can.

If my income doubled, what would I do differently? ______________________________

If my income doubled, what would still be the same? ____________________

What would I still worry about? ____________________

What would I still want? ____________________

What does this reveal about the relationship between more money and contentment?

Part C: The "When/Then" Trap

Complete these sentences with your automatic thoughts.

When I have ______________________________, then I will feel secure.

When I have ______________________________, then I will feel successful.

When I have ______________________________, then I will feel free.

When I have ______________________________, then I will feel worthy.

When I have ______________________________, then I will be happy.

Now, reflect on a past "when/then" you have already achieved.

A "when/then" I once believed: ____

When I achieved it, I felt: ____

How long did that feeling last? ____

What did I want next? ____

What does this teach me? ____

____

____

Part D: Defining Your "Enough"

There is no universal "enough." It must be defined by each person, in their own context, according to their own values.

To feel secure, I need: ____

____

To feel free, I need: ______________________________

____

To live well, I need: ______________________________

____

To be generous, I need: ______________________________

____

To be at peace, I need: ______________________________

____

My "enough" number (if you have one): $______________________________

My "enough" lifestyle (describe): ____

____

____

____

EXERCISE 9.3: FINANCIAL ANXIETY RELEASE

What Are You Carrying That Isn't Yours to Hold?

____

Part A: The Worry Inventory

List the financial worries that currently occupy your mind.

Worry	On a scale of 1-10, how much energy does this consume?	Is this worry within my control?	Can I take action on this today?
1.		☐ Yes ☐ No ☐ Partially	☐ Yes ☐ No
2.		☐ Yes ☐ No ☐ Partially	☐ Yes ☐ No
3.		☐ Yes ☐ No ☐ Partially	☐ Yes ☐ No
4.		☐ Yes ☐ No ☐ Partially	☐ Yes ☐ No
5.		☐ Yes ☐ No ☐ Partially	☐ Yes ☐ No
6.		☐ Yes ☐ No ☐ Partially	☐ Yes ☐ No

Part B: The Serenity Prayer for Finances

"God, grant me the serenity to accept the things I cannot change, courage to change the things I can, and wisdom to know the difference."

Apply this to your financial worries.

Things I CANNOT change about my financial situation (acceptance):

1. ____________________
2. ____________________
3. ____________________

What would it mean to truly accept these? ____________________

____

Things I CAN change or influence (courage):

1. ____________________
2. ____________________
3. ____________________

What is one small action I will take this week on something I can change? ____________________

Part C: The Release Statement

Choose one financial worry you have been carrying. Write a statement releasing it.

The worry I release today is: ____

I have held this worry because: ____

Holding this worry has cost me: ____

Releasing this worry does not mean I don't care. It means I am choosing not to carry what I cannot control.

I release this worry to:

☐ God ☐ Time ☐ The universe ☐ My future self ☐ Other:

____

Today, I choose to put down this weight.

Signed: ______________________ **Date:** ____________

Part D: Ritual of Release (Optional)

Consider a symbolic act to mark your release.

My release ritual: ______________________________________

Date completed: ________________________________

How I felt afterward: ______________________________________

EXERCISE 9.4: CONTENTMENT AS A SKILL – LEARNING TO WANT WHAT YOU HAVE

The Discipline of Enough

Part A: Contentment Practices Inventory

Check any practices you already use to cultivate contentment.

☐ Keeping a gratitude journal

☐ Regularly unsubscribing from marketing emails

☐ Taking a "fast" from shopping or social media

☐ Spending time in nature

☐ Practicing mindfulness or meditation

☐ Volunteering or serving others

☐ Reading philosophy, scripture, or wisdom literature

☐ Having conversations about values, not possessions

☐ Living below my means intentionally

☐ Celebrating others' successes without comparison

☐ Other: ____

____

Part B: Designing Your Contentment Practice

Choose one contentment practice to develop over the next 30 days.

My chosen practice: ____

____

When/How often I will practice: ____

What I hope to learn: ____

____

How I will track my progress: ____

Part C: The Contentment Muscle – Small Experiments

Try one of these experiments this week.

Experiment	What I Did	What I Noticed
The Possession Pause – Before buying something non-essential, wait 48 hours and ask: "Do I need this, or am I just wanting?"		
The Gratitude Substitute – When you feel envy or desire, immediately name three things you're grateful for.		
The "Good Enough" Purchase – Deliberately buy the "good enough" version, not the premium. Notice how it feels.		

Experiment	What I Did	What I Noticed
The Unsubscribe Spree – Unsubscribe from 5 retail emails. Notice if you miss them.		
The Comparison Fast – Spend one full day without checking social media or comparing yourself to anyone.		

EXERCISE 9.5: THE FINANCIAL SABBATH

Rest from Worry and Wanting

Part A: Understanding Sabbath for Your Finances

The principle of Sabbath is not just about rest from work; it is rest from striving, acquiring, and worrying.

What would a "financial Sabbath" look like for you?

☐ One day with no spending

☐ One day with no checking financial accounts

☐ One day with no financial worry (intentional)

☐ One day with no comparison/consumption

☐ One day dedicated to gratitude and reflection

☐ Other:

____

____

Part B: Designing Your Financial Sabbath

My financial Sabbath practice:

Day of week: ____________________________________

Duration: ☐ 2 hours ☐ Half day ☐ Full day ☐ 24 hours

Boundaries I will set:

☐ No purchases (except absolute essentials)

☐ No checking bank/investment accounts

☐ No financial news or media

☐ No comparison/social media

☐ No financial conversations (except gratitude)

What I will do instead: ____

____

What I hope to experience: ____

____

____

Part C: Financial Sabbath Reflection

Complete after your first financial Sabbath.

Date of Sabbath: ____

What was hardest about this practice? ____

____

What was most life-giving? ____

What did I notice about my relationship with money when I stepped back? ______________________________

What did I notice about myself? ______________________________

Will I continue this practice? ☐ Yes ☐ No ☐ Modified version

EXERCISE 9.6: THE COMPARISON DETOX

Breaking the Gaze

Part A: The Comparison Thermometer

On a scale of 1-10, how much does social comparison affect your financial contentment today?

1 ☐ 2 ☐ 3 ☐ 4 ☐ 5 ☐ 6 ☐ 7 ☐ 8 ☐ 9 ☐ 10 ☐

(1 = "Not at all," 10 = "It dominates my thinking")

What are your primary comparison domains? ______________________________

____

Who are your primary comparison targets? ______________________________

____

____

Part B: The Cost of Comparison – Revisited

What has comparison cost you in the past month?

Cost Type	Specific Examples
Financial	

Cost Type	Specific Examples
Emotional	
Relational	
Time	
Spiritual	

Part C: Comparison Interrupts

Design specific responses when comparison thoughts arise.

Comparison Trigger	My Interrupt Script
Example: Seeing someone's luxury vacation on social media	"I don't know their full story. I am grateful for my own travels."

Comparison Trigger	My Interrupt Script

Part D: The 7-Day Comparison Fast

I commit to a 7-day comparison fast from __________ to ______________________.

During this fast, I will:

☐ Avoid social media entirely

☐ Unfollow/mute specific accounts

☐ Redirect comparison thoughts when they arise

☐ Practice gratitude immediately after envy

☐ Other:

____

Post-Fast Reflection:

What was the hardest part? ____

What did I learn about myself? ______________________________

What shift, if any, occurred in my financial contentment? ______________________________

EXERCISE 9.7: PEACE – THE ULTIMATE METRIC

Measuring What Matters

Part A: Redefining Financial Success

What if peace, not net worth, were the primary metric of financial health?

On a scale of 1-10, how much financial peace do I experience right now?

1 ☐ 2 ☐ 3 ☐ 4 ☐ 5 ☐ 6 ☐ 7 ☐ 8 ☐ 9 ☐ 10 ☐

What contributes to this peace? ______________________________

____

What diminishes this peace? ______________________________

____

____

Part B: The Peace Portfolio

What assets (financial and non-financial) contribute to your sense of financial peace?

Peace Asset	How It Contributes to Peace
Financial (e.g., emergency fund, low debt, insurance)	
Psychological (e.g., contentment practice, gratitude)	
Social (e.g., trusted advisors, supportive community)	
Spiritual (e.g., faith, trust in providence)	

Part C: One Action to Increase Peace This Week

The one thing that would most increase my financial peace right now is:

The smallest possible step toward this is: ______________________________________

I will take this step on: ______________________________

BEHAVIORAL PRACTICE: 7-DAY CONTENTMENT AND GRATITUDE EXPERIMENT

Experiment Choice (choose one):

☐ **Experiment A: The Daily Gratitude Ledger** – Each evening, write three specific financial or non-financial gratitudes. Do not miss a day.

☐ **Experiment B: The Comparison Fast** – Seven days with no social media, or no financial comparison of any kind. Journal the experience.

☐ **Experiment C: The Financial Sabbath** – Observe one full day of financial rest (no spending, no checking accounts, no worry). Repeat at least twice during the week.

☐ **Experiment D: The "Enough" Audit** – Each day, identify one moment when you felt "enough" – a moment of sufficiency and contentment. Journal it.

Daily Log

Day	Experiment Activity	Gratitude/Insight	Challenge Encountered	Peace Level (1-10)
1				
2				
3				

Day	Experiment Activity	Gratitude/Insight	Challenge Encountered	Peace Level (1-10)
4				
5				
6				
7				

End-of-Week Reflection

What was the most powerful moment of this experiment? ______________________________

What did I learn about my capacity for contentment? ______________________________

What resistance to gratitude did I encounter? ______________________________

____

What surprised me? ______________________________

____

One practice I will continue: ______________________________

____

____

EXERCISE 9.8: CONTENTMENT IN ALL CIRCUMSTANCES

Learning the Secret

Part A: The Apostle Paul's Testimony

"I have learned in whatever situation I am to be content. I know how to be brought low, and I know how to abound. In any and every circumstance, I have learned the secret of facing plenty and hunger, abundance and need." (Philippians 4:11-12)

Paul says contentment is LEARNED. It is not a personality trait; it is a discipline.

What circumstances have been your teachers of contentment?

Circumstance	What It Taught Me
Times of scarcity/loss	

Circumstance	What It Taught Me
Times of abundance/gain	

What is the "secret" Paul discovered? ______________________________

____

____

Part B: Contentment in Scarcity

If I experienced financial loss or prolonged hardship, what would I still have that cannot be taken?

____

____

____

What would I still be? ____

____

____

Part C: Contentment in Abundance

If I experienced significant financial gain, what would I need to guard against to maintain contentment?

____

____

____

What practices would I need to maintain? ____

____

____

FAITH INTEGRATION

Learning Contentment from the One Who Provides

Scripture Meditation

"*I have learned to be content whatever the circumstances.*" (Philippians 4:11)

"*The Lord is my shepherd; I shall not want.*" (Psalm 23:1)

"*Keep your life free from love of money, and be content with what you have, for he has said, 'I will never leave you nor forsake you.'*" (Hebrews 13:5)

"*Better is a little with the fear of the Lord than great treasure and trouble with it.*" (Proverbs 15:16)

"*Do not lay up for yourselves treasures on earth, where moth and rust destroy and where thieves break in and steal, but lay up for yourselves treasures in heaven.*" (Matthew 6:19-20)

Part A: God as Source

Where do I look for security, satisfaction, and worth – in God or in money?

____

____

What would change if I truly believed that God is my source, not my paycheck or portfolio?

____

____

____

Part B: Contentment as Trust

Contentment is not resignation; it is trust in the character and provision of God.

What does my discontent reveal about what I believe about God? ____

____

____

What does my gratitude reveal about what I believe about God? ____

____

____

____

Part C: Prayer for Contentment

Write a prayer asking God to teach you the secret of contentment.

____

____

Part D: The Peace That Passes Understanding

"And the peace of God, which surpasses all understanding, will guard your hearts and your minds in Christ Jesus." (Philippians 4:7)

This peace is not dependent on circumstances. It is a gift.

I receive this peace today. I release the anxiety I have been carrying.

Amen.

CHAPTER 9 ACTION PLAN

One gratitude practice I will integrate into my daily life:

One financial worry I am releasing (and to whom/where):

One comparison trigger I will eliminate or reduce:

One contentment experiment I will conduct this month:

One financial Sabbath I will observe this month:

One truth to remember:

"I have learned to be content whatever the circumstances." (Philippians 4:11)

CHAPTER 9 COMPLETION CHECKLIST

☐ I have listed 10 things money cannot buy

☐ I have completed the 7-day gratitude ledger

☐ I have written a gratitude letter (or draft)

☐ I have completed the Contentment Diagnostic

☐ I have defined my personal "enough"

☐ I have written a financial worry release statement

☐ I have designed and practiced a financial Sabbath

☐ I have attempted a comparison fast or detox

☐ I have completed the 7-day behavioral experiment

☐ I have engaged with the faith integration reflection

☐ I am ready to proceed to the next chapter

Date Completed: ____

My Key Insight from Chapter 9:

____

____

____

____

"Contentment is not the fulfillment of what you want, but the realization of how much you already have. It is not the absence of desire, but the presence of gratitude. It is not the end of striving, but the discovery that what you have been striving for has already been given. The secret of contentment is not having more; it is wanting what you have."

CHAPTER 10

The Future of Money Psychology

Navigating AI, Digital Money, Ethics, and Uncertainty

Learning Objectives

☐ Understand the psychological dynamics of human-AI collaboration in financial decisions
☐ Recognize how digital payment systems affect spending behavior and develop counter-strategies
☐ Identify ethical pitfalls in fintech and build personal ethical defense practices
☐ Manage the mental health implications of constant financial connectivity
☐ Cultivate adaptability and preparedness for an uncertain financial future

☐ Integrate timeless wisdom with emerging technology for financial sovereignty

---

Key Concepts Review

Term	Definition	In My Own Words
Automation Bias	Over-reliance on automated systems, trusting machine output even when it conflicts with evidence	
Algorithm Aversion	Rejecting algorithmic advice after a single mistake, even when it outperforms humans overall	
Explainable AI (XAI)	Artificial intelligence designed to provide understandable rationales for its decisions	

Term	Definition	In My Own Words
Choice Architecture	The design of environments in which people make decisions; shapes choices without forbidding options	
Dark Patterns	Interface designs deliberately crafted to trick, manipulate, or deceive users	
Pain of Paying	The psychological discomfort associated with parting with money; varies by payment method	
Payment Decoupling	The separation of the pleasure of acquisition from the pain of payment, enabling frictionless spending	
Zombie Money	Recurring payments for unused subscriptions; funds	

Term	Definition	In My Own Words
	that leave your account invisibly	
Data Sovereignty	The right to control one's own personal data, especially financial information	
Moral Crumple Zone	When a human bears the blame for an algorithmic failure, diffusing accountability from designers	
Adaptation Portfolio	Personal assets that generate new resources in changing conditions: skills, network, liquidity	
Tolerance for Uncertainty	The capacity to function and decide without complete information; a learnable psychological muscle	

Term	Definition	In My Own Words
Future Time Perspective	The habitual focus on past, present, or future consequences; adaptive flexibility is key	
Algorithmic Intelligence	The ability to interrogate, collaborate with, and appropriately override algorithmic systems	

EXERCISE 10.1: HUMAN-AI COLLABORATION – DEFINING YOUR PARTNERSHIP

Who Does What?

Part A: Your Current AI Exposure

List all the AI-driven financial tools you currently use or encounter.

Tool/App	What It Does	Do I Understand How It Works? (1-5)	Do I Trust It? (1-5)	Have I Ever Overridden It?
Example: Robo-advisor	Manages my IRA, recommends allocation	3	4	No
1.				

Tool/App	What It Does	Do I Understand How It Works? (1-5)	Do I Trust It? (1-5)	Have I Ever Overridden It?
2.				
3.				
4.				
5.				

Part B: Automation Bias Self-Assessment

Rate each statement honestly (1 = Strongly Disagree, 5 = Strongly Agree).

Statement	1	2	3	4	5
I assume my banking/investment app's recommendations are correct.	☐	☐	☐	☐	☐
I rarely question automated savings or investment suggestions.	☐	☐	☐	☐	☐
I've followed an app's advice even when it felt wrong.	☐	☐	☐	☐	☐
I find it mentally exhausting to double-check algorithmic outputs.	☐	☐	☐	☐	☐

Statement	1	2	3	4	5
I believe the algorithms I use are more objective than humans.	☐	☐	☐	☐	☐

Reflection: Do you tend toward automation bias? Where might this be costing you?

____

____

____

Part C: Algorithm Aversion Self-Assessment

Statement	1	2	3	4	5
One mistake by an algorithm makes me lose trust completely.	☐	☐	☐	☐	☐

Statement	1	2	3	4	5
I trust a human advisor's gut feeling more than an AI's calculation.	☐	☐	☐	☐	☐
I feel a sense of betrayal when a machine gets it wrong.	☐	☐	☐	☐	☐
I prefer imperfect human judgment to algorithmic precision.	☐	☐	☐	☐	☐

Reflection: Do you have algorithm aversion? How might this limit you?

____

____

____

Part D: Your Human-AI Collaboration Constitution

Define the domains and rules of your partnership with financial AI.

AI-PRIMARY DOMAIN (Execution & Surveillance) – I let the algorithm run on autopilot:

1. ______________________________
2. ______________________________
3. ______________________________

Example: Rebalancing my portfolio to target allocations quarterly.

HUMAN-PRIMARY DOMAIN (Values & Judgment) – I retain exclusive authority:

1. ______________________________
2. ______________________________
3. ______________________________

Example: Deciding what my financial goals are, what "enough" means, ethical red lines.

COLLABORATIVE DOMAIN (Analysis & Recommendation) – AI advises, I decide:

1. ______________________________
2. ______________________________
3. ______________________________

Example: Running 1,000 simulations of retirement scenarios; I choose which scenario matches my risk tolerance.

Part E: The "Why" Checkpoint – My Quarterly Review Protocol

Every quarter, when my AI system presents a recommendation, I will ask:

☐ "Why are you recommending this?"
☐ "What data and assumptions is this based on?"
☐ "What are the limitations or risks you're not showing me?"
☐ "Does this align with my life goals and values, not just my financial metrics?"

If the system cannot provide a clear, logical rationale, I will:

☐ Not follow the recommendation
☐ Seek a second opinion (human or different AI)
☐ Investigate further before acting

Part F: Override Procedures – My Emergency Brake

I will override the algorithm under these conditions:

☐ Values Violation Override:

"If the algorithm recommends investing in companies that violate my ethical standards (list: ________________________________), I will override it, regardless of projected return."

☐ Life Event Override:

"Upon a major life event (marriage, childbirth, job loss, inheritance, serious illness), I will pause ALL automated investing

and saving rules for ____ days and re-evaluate from first principles."

☐ **Unprecedented Condition Override:**

"If market conditions exceed historical parameters (e.g., VIX > ____, Fed funds rate ____, geopolitical event without precedent), I will switch to my pre-defined crisis protocol."

My Crisis Protocol (brief description): ______________________________

____

____

EXERCISE 10.2: DIGITAL PAYMENT SYSTEMS – RE-EMBODYING MONEY

Restoring the Pain of Paying

Part A: Your Payment Method Profile

What payment methods do you use most frequently? Rank by frequency (1 = most often).

☐ Cash
☐ Debit card
☐ Credit card

☐ Digital wallet (Apple Pay, Google Pay)
☐ One-click online payment (Amazon, etc.)
☐ Buy Now, Pay Later (Afterpay, Klarna)
☐ Peer-to-peer apps (Venmo, Zelle, CashApp)
☐ Automatic recurring payments

How does each method affect your sense of "spending money"?

Method	Does It Feel "Real"? (1-5)	Do You Track It Easily? (1-5)	Do You Overspend With It? (1-5)
Cash			
Debit			
Credit			
Digital wallet			
One-click			
BNPL			

Method	Does It Feel "Real"? (1-5)	Do You Track It Easily? (1-5)	Do You Overspend With It? (1-5)
P2P			
Auto-pay			

Part B: Friction Reintroduction – Your Speed Bump Design

Choose strategies to insert friction into your spending.

☐ **The 24-Hour Rule:** For any non-essential online purchase over $_____, I will wait 24 hours before purchasing.

☐ **Remove Saved Payment Info:** I will delete stored credit cards from:

☐ Amazon ☐ Apple/Google Pay ☐ My browser ☐ Other apps: ___________

☐ **Separate "Frictionful" Account:** I will open a separate account for discretionary spending with:

☐ No debit card ☐ No digital wallet access ☐ 1-3 day transfer delay

☐ **Cash-Only Categories:** I will use cash for these spending categories:

1. ______________________ 2. ______________________ 3. ______________________

☐ **Credit Card Relegation:** I will use credit cards ONLY for:

☐ Pre-planned, budgeted purchases ☐ Purchases with rewards I actually use ☐ Emergencies only

☐ **Digital Wallet Containment:** I will use Apple Pay/Google Pay ONLY for:

☐ Public transit ☐ One specific subscription ☐ Other: _______________

Part C: Digital Envelope System Design

Recreate the psychological power of cash envelopes digitally.

My chosen tool: ☐ Bank with sub-accounts (e.g., Ally, Monzo) ☐ Budgeting app (e.g., YNAB, Mvelopes) ☐ Manual spreadsheet

My digital envelopes:

Envelope Name	Monthly Budget	Current Balance	Last Funded Date
	$	$	
	$	$	
	$	$	
	$	$	
	$	$	

My "Envelope Zero" Rule: When an envelope balance reaches $0, I:

☐ Stop spending in that category for the month
☐ Hold a "budget committee meeting" with myself/partner before transferring from another envelope

My Mental Transaction Practice: Before any discretionary purchase, I will:

1. Check the relevant envelope balance.
2. If sufficient funds, complete purchase.
3. IMMEDIATELY log into my bank/app and transfer the amount from envelope to spending account.

Part D: Transaction Mindfulness Rituals

Choose rituals to reconnect your consciousness to your spending.

☐ **The Three-Breath Pause:** Before tapping "Confirm" or the payment sensor, I will take three slow, deep breaths and ask: *"Is this aligned with my values and goals?"*

☐ **Verbalize the Exchange:** I will silently (or aloud) state: *"I am exchanging $_____ of my life energy for this."*

☐ **Evening Transaction Review:** Each evening, I will spend 5 minutes reviewing the day's digital transactions in my banking app—not just scanning, but acknowledging each outflow.

☐ **Weekly Balance Broadcast:** I will set up a weekly text/email from my bank with my checking balance and total discretionary spending.

☐ **Subscription Audit Day:** I will schedule a recurring quarterly "Subscription Audit" on: __________ (date)

Part E: Zombie Money Hunt

List all your recurring subscriptions and memberships.

Service	Cost/Month	Last Used Date	Keep? (Y/N)	Cancellation Date
	$			
	$			
	$			
	$			
	$			
	$			
	$			

Total monthly zombie money: $________

Total annual zombie money: $________

What could this money become in 10 years at 7%? $________ *(estimate)*

EXERCISE 10.3: ETHICAL FINTECH – BECOMING A CONSCIOUS CONSUMER

Your Digital Rights and Responsibilities

Part A: Personal Ethical Fintech Audit

Before using any new financial app or service, complete this checklist.

App/Service Name: ______________________________

☐ **Dark Pattern Scan:**

Red Flag	Present?	Notes
Desired actions (sign up, buy) are bright/large; cautious options are gray/tiny	☐ Yes ☐ No	
Easier to subscribe than to unsubscribe	☐ Yes ☐ No	

Red Flag	Present?	Notes
Emotionally manipulative language ("Don't miss out!")	☐ Yes ☐ No	
Confusing menus for privacy settings	☐ Yes ☐ No	
"Free trial" requires credit card; unclear when billing starts	☐ Yes ☐ No	

If I detect manipulation, I will: ☐ Not use this service ☐ Proceed with extreme caution

---

☐ **Transparency Test:**

Question	Answer Found?	Is It Clear?
What is the full fee schedule/APR/all potential costs?	☐ Yes ☐ No	☐ Yes ☐ No

Question	Answer Found?	Is It Clear?
Is there a clear, concise privacy policy in plain English?	☐ Yes ☐ No	☐ Yes ☐ No
What data do they collect?	☐ Yes ☐ No	☐ Yes ☐ No
Who do they share it with?	☐ Yes ☐ No	☐ Yes ☐ No
For robo-advisors: Do they explain their methodology and limitations?	☐ Yes ☐ No	☐ Yes ☐ No

Overall transparency grade: A B C D F

☐ "Worst-Case" Scenario Check:

Question	Answer Found?	Is Process Humane?
How do I dispute a charge?	☐ Yes ☐ No	☐ Yes ☐ No
How do I close my account?	☐ Yes ☐ No	☐ Yes ☐ No
Is there a phone number or live chat for support?	☐ Yes ☐ No	☐ Yes ☐ No

Red flags: ____

Part B: Your Personal Data Valuation Framework

Stop treating data sharing as binary. Create your data sharing tiers.

TIER 1 – NON-NEGOTIABLE, NEVER SHARE:

☐ Full transaction history linked to my identity (for advertising)
☐ Social Security number (beyond absolute legal necessity)
☐ Biometric data for non-essential purposes
☐ Other: ____

TIER 2 – HIGH VALUE, REQUIRE HIGH RETURN:

☐ Investment goals and risk tolerance (only for fiduciary advisors)
☐ Income and spending patterns (only for tools that save me more than the data is worth)
☐ Other: ____

TIER 3 – LOW VALUE, CAN BE TRADED:

☐ Anonymous, aggregated spending data
☐ Basic demographic info for genuinely useful free services
☐ Other: ____

Part C: Data Minimalism – My Hygiene Practices

When signing up for new services:

☐ I will ask: "What is the minimum data I need to share to get the core benefit?"
☐ I will use dummy email addresses for trials (e.g., +fintech@mydomain.com)

☐ I will use virtual credit card numbers for merchants I don't fully trust

Quarterly Data Clean-Up:

☐ I will review connected apps in my bank account
☐ I will review permissions in Google/Facebook/Apple settings
☐ I will revoke access for anything unused
☐ Scheduled next clean-up: ______________________________

Part D: Algorithmic Fairness – My Accountability Rights

When an algorithm denies me credit, a loan, or a limit increase:

☐ I will ALWAYS request a human review.
☐ I will document my "data self" – a file of my financial reliability (timely payments, steady income, good habits).
☐ I will note the date, the company, and the outcome for potential follow-up.

Supporting Ethical Alt-FIs:

☐ I will research and consider: credit unions, B-Corp certified fintechs, community development financial institutions (CDFIs).

One ethical financial institution I will explore this month: ______________________________

Part E: Informed Consent – It's Not a One-Time Click

Annual Terms & Privacy Review:

Platform	Date of Last Review	Changes Noted?	Action Needed

Privacy-Focused Tools I Use:

☐ Browser: Brave / Firefox / Other: __________
☐ Search engine: DuckDuckGo / Other: __________
☐ Email: ProtonMail / Tutanota / Other: __________
☐ VPN: __________

EXERCISE 10.4: MENTAL HEALTH AND FINTECH – PROTECTING YOUR PSYCHOLOGICAL SOVEREIGNTY

Digital Wellbeing Practices

Part A: The Notification Purge

List all financial apps and the notifications you will disable.

App	Current Notifications	New Setting	Date Changed
Banking app			
Investing app			
Budgeting app			
Credit card app			

App	Current Notifications	New Setting	Date Changed
Payment apps			
Other:			

My Sacred Check-In Times:

☐ I will check my budget: ___________ (day/time)
☐ I will check investments: ___________ (frequency)
☐ I will NOT check finances: ☐ In the bedroom ☐ After ____ PM ☐ First hour of waking

---

Part B: Financial Stress Monitoring – Know Your Triggers

The "Spending & Feeling" Log – 7-Day Trial

Day	Purchase/Financial Task	Emotional Tag (Before)	Emotional Tag (After)	Physical Sensation
1				

Day	Purchase/Financial Task	Emotional Tag (Before)	Emotional Tag (After)	Physical Sensation
2				
3				
4				
5				
6				
7				

Emotional Tag Options: Anxious, Guilty, Empowered, Joyful, Obligated, Proud, Fearful, Indifferent, Ashamed, Relieved, Regretful, Other

Patterns I notice: ____

____

____

Part C: Physical Symptom Alerts

Before opening any financial app, I will do a 10-second body scan.

Checkpoint	Yes	No
Is my jaw tight?	☐	☐
Are my shoulders up at my ears?	☐	☐
Is my breath shallow?	☐	☐
Is my stomach knotted?	☐	☐

If ANY are "Yes," my intervention is:

☐ 3 minutes of diaphragmatic breathing (4-7-8 or box breathing)
☐ 5-minute walk away from screen
☐ Drink a glass of water slowly
☐ Other:

Then I may proceed, or I may reschedule the financial task.

Part D: Circuit-Breaker Rules

Write your pre-commitments for high-stress financial moments.

If my investment portfolio is down more than ____% in a day/week:

I will NOT open the app. Instead, I will:

____

If I feel the urge to engage in "retail therapy" due to stress:

I will NOT shop. Instead, I will:

____

If I feel overwhelmed by financial complexity:

I will NOT avoid. Instead, I will:

____

____

Part E: Digital Detox – Reclaiming Analog Space

☐ The Quarterly Financial Sabbath

I will observe a financial technology fast one weekend per quarter.

Quarter	Dates	What I Did Instead	How I Felt
Q1			
Q2			
Q3			
Q4			

☐ **The "Paper Month" (Annual)**

I will conduct one month of paper-based budget tracking.

Scheduled month: ____________________________________

Materials needed: notebook, envelopes, calculator, pen

☐ **Tech-Free Financial Rituals**

I will pair financial tasks with analog pleasures:

Financial Task	Analog Pleasure
Example: Monthly net worth review	Cup of tea, favorite chair, instrumental music

Financial Task	Analog Pleasure

EXERCISE 10.5: PREPARING FOR AN UNCERTAIN FINANCIAL FUTURE

Building Your Expedition Kit

Part A: Your Future Time Perspective (FTP) Profile

Where do you typically focus? Rank the time horizons you think about most (1 = most frequent).

☐ Days – Immediate needs, today's expenses
☐ Months – This month's bills, near-term goals
☐ Years – Next 1-5 years, major purchases
☐ Decades – Retirement, children's education
☐ Generations – Legacy, impact beyond my life

What are the strengths of your dominant time horizon? ______________________________

What are the blind spots? ________________________________

____

What would it mean to cultivate a "balanced telescope" – the ability to shift between time horizons as needed?

____

____

____

Part B: Tolerance for Uncertainty – Self-Assessment

Statement	1 (Strongly Disagree) – 5 (Strongly Agree)
I need clear answers before I can make decisions.	1 2 3 4 5
I can function well even when the future is ambiguous.	1 2 3 4 5

Statement	1 (Strongly Disagree) – 5 (Strongly Agree)
Not knowing what will happen makes me anxious.	1 2 3 4 5
I view uncertainty as an opportunity, not a threat.	1 2 3 4 5
I prefer a rigid plan over a flexible framework.	1 2 3 4 5

My uncertainty tolerance is: ☐ Low ☐ Moderate ☐ High

One small practice I will try to stretch my uncertainty muscle: ______________________________

____

____

Part C: The Three Futures Ritual

Once a year, sketch three plausible, divergent financial worlds for 15 years from now.

Future A: The Continuation (Current trends accelerate)

- Technology: ____
- Economy: ____
- Skills/assets that thrive: __________________________________
- Skills/assets that decline: ________________________________
- What "financial security" means: ____________________________

Future B: The Reversion (Backlash, deglobalization, return to tangible)

- Technology: ____
- Economy: ____
- Skills/assets that thrive: __________________________________
- Skills/assets that decline: ________________________________
- What "financial security" means: ____________________________

Future C: The Transformation (Post-scarcity breakthrough, societal shift)

- Technology: ____
- Economy: ____

- Skills/assets that thrive: ____
- Skills/assets that decline: ____
- What "financial security" means: ______________________________________

Scheduled date for next Three Futures Ritual: ___________

Part D: Your Adaptation Portfolio

Your capacity to generate new resources, no matter what happens.

SKILL CAPITAL – My T-Shaped Profile

Deep Expertise (Vertical)	Adjacent, Adaptable Skills (Horizontal)
1.	1.
2.	2.
3.	3.

One new skill I will invest in this year (for adaptability): ____

How I will invest (time/money): ____________________

____

NETWORK CAPITAL – My Expedition Crew

Not just powerful people, but curious, kind, resourceful people from different fields.

People who give me early warnings / different perspectives:

1. ____________________
2. ____________________

People I can collaborate with on unexpected projects:

1. ____________________
2. ____________________

People who provide support when I hit a dead end:

1. ____________________
2. ____________________

One network-building action I will take this month: ____________________

____

LIQUIDITY & OPTIONALITY – My Financial Fuel for Agility

Asset	Current Amount	Target Amount	Accessibility (1-5)	Purpose
Emergency fund	$	$		Survival buffer
Career transition fund	$	$		Retraining, sabbatical
Opportunity fund	$	$		Say "yes" to surprises
Other:	$	$		

Part E: Uncertainty Management System

MEASURABLE RISKS (Known-Knowns) – Use traditional tools

Risk	Tool (Insurance, EF, Diversification)	Status
Market correction		
Job loss in my field		
Major car repair		
Health emergency		
Other:		

DEEP UNCERTAINTY (Unknown-Unknowns) – Rely on Adaptation Portfolio

Uncertainty	How My Skill/ Network/ Liquidity Helps
Technology makes my profession obsolete	

Uncertainty	How My Skill/ Network/ Liquidity Helps
Hyperinflationary event	
Social redefinition of wealth	
Other:	

Part F: Pre-Mortem for Your Financial Plan

Assume your central financial plan has failed catastrophically in 20 years. Why?

My plan: ____
–

It is 20 years from now. The plan failed because:

1. ____
2. ____
3. ____
4. ____
5. ____

What hidden assumptions did this reveal? ______________________________

____

What one hedge or buffer will I add to my plan? ______________________________

____

____

Part G: Scenario-Based Decision Making

When facing a major financial decision, evaluate it against your Three Futures.

Decision under consideration: ______________________________

Scenario	How This Decision Would Fare	Notes
Future A (Continuation)		
Future B (Reversion)		

Scenario	How This Decision Would Fare	Notes
Future (Transformation)	C	

Does this decision increase or decrease my overall adaptability across possible futures?

☐ Increases adaptability ☐ Decreases adaptability ☐ Neutral / Mixed

What can I do to hedge this decision (increase adaptability regardless of which future emerges)?

____

____

Part H: Horizon Scanning – Becoming a Lookout

My "Weak Signals" Feed: I will follow thinkers/publications from:

☐ Fringe technology ☐ Sociology ☐ Climate science ☐ Philosophy ☐ Other: ________

Sources I will add: ____

The Quarterly "What's Changing?" Review:

☐ Scheduled for: ____________ (quarterly recurring)

Questions I will ask:

- What has changed in the world that might, in 5-10 years, affect what my skills are worth?
- What has changed that might affect what my assets are worth?
- What has changed that might affect what a good life costs?

BEHAVIORAL PRACTICE: 7-DAY FUTURE-READY EXPERIMENT

Experiment Choice (choose one):

☐ **Experiment A: The Friction Audit** – For 7 days, track every digital payment. Note the emotional "pain" (1-10). Identify one area to add friction. Implement on day 8.

☐ **Experiment B: The Notification Purge** – Disable all non-essential financial notifications. Observe changes in anxiety and financial awareness.

☐ **Experiment C: The Three Futures Mini-Exercise** – Spend 15 minutes each day imagining one of the three futures (rotate). Journal how it feels and what it suggests.

☐ **Experiment D: The Human Override** – Identify one area where you currently use automation. This week, consciously override or question it. Journal the experience.

☐ **Experiment E: The Ethical Fintech Audit** – Audit one financial app you use using the framework in 10.3. Decide whether to keep it, modify settings, or leave.

Daily Log

Day	Experiment Activity	What I Noticed	Emotional State	Insight for Future Readiness
1				
2				
3				
4				

Day	Experiment Activity	What I Noticed	Emotional State	Insight for Future Readiness
5				
6				
7				

End-of-Week Reflection

What was the most challenging moment? ________________________________

What was the most surprising discovery? ________________________________

What skill, practice, or perspective do I want to develop further? ________________________________

One practice I will continue: ____

FAITH INTEGRATION

Wisdom for an Algorithmic Age

Scripture Meditation

"*Trust in the Lord with all your heart, and do not lean on your own understanding. In all your ways acknowledge him, and he will make straight your paths.*" (Proverbs 3:5-6)

"*For which of you, desiring to build a tower, does not first sit down and count the cost, whether he has enough to complete it?*" (Luke 14:28)

"*Do not be conformed to this world, but be transformed by the renewal of your mind, that by testing you may discern what is the will of God, what is good and acceptable and perfect.*" (Romans 12:2)

"*The heart of man plans his way, but the Lord establishes his steps.*" (Proverbs 16:9)

Part A: Trust, Technology, and Providence

Where do I place my ultimate trust – in algorithms, institutions, or God?

What financial technologies have I treated as infallible? ______________________________

What would it mean to "not lean on my own understanding" while still using the best tools available?

Part B: Stewardship in an Age of AI

If everything I have is entrusted to me by God, how does that change my relationship with financial algorithms?

What ethical red lines does my faith draw that I will not let any algorithm cross?

Part C: Peace in Uncertainty

"Do not be anxious about tomorrow, for tomorrow will be anxious for itself. Sufficient for the day is its own trouble." (Matthew 6:34)

How does this command intersect with prudent planning for an uncertain future?

What anxiety about the financial future do I need to release today? ______________________________

I release this to: ☐ God ☐ Time ☐ My future self ☐ Other: ______________________________

Part D: Prayer for the Future-Ready Steward

Write a prayer asking for wisdom, discernment, and courage for the financial future.

CHAPTER 10 ACTION PLAN

One change I will make to my human-AI collaboration:

One friction I will reintroduce to my digital spending:

One ethical fintech practice I will adopt:

One digital wellbeing boundary I will set:

One element I will add to my Adaptation Portfolio (skill, network, liquidity):

One truth to remember:

"The most valuable asset you will ever possess is not in your brokerage account, but between your ears and in the connections of your heart."

CHAPTER 10 COMPLETION CHECKLIST

☐ I have completed the Human-AI Collaboration Constitution
☐ I have defined my override procedures
☐ I have audited my payment methods and designed friction strategies
☐ I have created a digital envelope system or plan
☐ I have conducted at least one ethical fintech audit
☐ I have defined my personal data valuation tiers
☐ I have completed a notification purge
☐ I have practiced the "Spending & Feeling" log or body scan
☐ I have scheduled a Three Futures Ritual
☐ I have assessed my Adaptation Portfolio
☐ I have conducted a pre-mortem on my financial plan
☐ I have completed the 7-day behavioral experiment
☐ I have engaged with the faith integration reflection
☐ I am ready to proceed to the Conclusion

Date Completed: ______________________________

My Key Insight from Chapter 10:

"You are the shipbuilder and the explorer. The waters ahead are uncharted. Do not waste your life building a perfect dock for a sea that is already receding. Build a resilient vessel. Pack a versatile kit. Gather a steadfast crew. And then, with eyes wide open to the horizon and to your own capable hands, set sail. The future is not a destination to be reached. It is an ocean to be navigated, and your preparedness is the wind in your sails."

CONCLUSION

The Integration: Where Your Financial Psychology Meets the Future's Edge

---

Learning Objectives

☐ Understand the two modes of financial being – Technologist and Philosopher-Psychologist – and how to integrate them
☐ Assess your current Financial Dual-Citizenship in the Digital Republic and the Republic of Inner Experience
☐ Identify personal gaps in the practices of continuous learning, unlearning, and re-centering
☐ Define financial maturity and articulate your vision of it
☐ Recognize yourself as the author of your ongoing financial narrative

☐ Create a personalized integration practice for lifelong financial wisdom

---

Key Concepts Review

Term	Definition	In My Own Words
The Technologist Mode	Engaging with the financial world as it is becoming; fluency in algorithms, digital platforms, data, and automation	
The Philosopher-Psychologist Mode	Grounding in timeless human needs, values, self-awareness, and meaning; questioning the ends of technology	
Financial Dual-Citizenship	Fluency and sovereignty in both the digital financial world and one's inner psychological domain	

Term	Definition	In My Own Words
Continuous Learning	Proactive, perpetual re-education in the architectures of money, technology, and behavior	
Continuous Unlearning	The courage to release outdated money scripts and assumptions that no longer serve	
Continuous Re-centering	Daily rituals that return attention to core values and inner peace amid financial complexity	
Peace Worth	The ultimate metric of financial success: the quality of mind one possesses while managing material life	

Term	Definition	In My Own Words
Financial Maturity	The capacity to move through the world of money with competence, clarity, and an unshakeable sense of being at home within oneself	
Author	The conscious, value-driven, feeling self who writes the ongoing story of one's financial life	

EXERCISE C.1: THE TWO MODES – SELF-ASSESSMENT

Where Are You Strong? Where Do You Need Integration?

Part A: The Technologist Mode – Your Digital Financial Fluency

Rate your current competency in each area (1 = "I don't know this at all," 5 = "I am confident and fluent").

Skill / Knowledge Area	Self-Rating (1-5)	I Want to Develop This (☐)
Understanding how my robo-advisor or investment app makes decisions		☐
Identifying dark patterns or manipulative design in financial apps		☐
Managing my digital financial security (passwords, 2FA, data sharing)		☐
Evaluating the credibility of a "finfluencer" or online financial advice		☐

Skill / Knowledge Area	Self-Rating (1-5)	I Want to Develop This (☐)
Using automation (savings, investing, bill pay) intentionally		☐
Basic understanding of how blockchain, crypto, or AI in finance works		☐
Reading and understanding a privacy policy or terms of service		☐
Using budgeting or tracking apps without becoming obsessive		☐
Participating in online financial communities with contributive intent		☐

My average Technologist score: ____ / 40

My greatest strength in this mode: ____________________

One skill I will develop next: ____________________

Part B: The Philosopher-Psychologist Mode – Your Inner Financial Sovereignty

Rate your current capacity in each area (1 = "Not like me at all," 5 = "This is deeply true of me").

Capacity / Practice	Self-Rating (1-5)	I Want to Develop This (☐)
I know my core financial triggers and scarcity wounds.		☐
I can sit with the anxiety of market volatility without impulsive action.		☐

Capacity / Practice	Self-Rating (1-5)	I Want to Develop This (☐)
My sense of security comes more from my resilience than my account balance.		☐
I regularly question whether my financial choices align with my values.		☐
I have a clear sense of "enough" for my life.		☐
I practice gratitude for non-financial forms of wealth.		☐
I can distinguish between acting from fear and acting from principle.		☐
I forgive myself for past financial mistakes and learn from them.		☐

Capacity / Practice	Self-Rating (1-5)	I Want to Develop This (☐)
I derive my self-worth from sources beyond net worth.		☐
I have a daily or weekly practice that reconnects me to what matters.		☐

My average Philosopher-Psychologist score: ____ / 50

My greatest strength in this mode: ______________________________

One capacity I will cultivate next: ______________________________

Part C: The Integration Gap

On a scale of 1-10, how integrated are these two modes in your daily financial life?

1 ☐ 2 ☐ 3 ☐ 4 ☐ 5 ☐ 6 ☐ 7 ☐ 8 ☐ 9 ☐ 10 ☐
(1 = "They operate in silos," 10 = "They are seamlessly woven together")

Describe a recent situation where you successfully integrated both modes:

Describe a recent situation where they were in conflict or one dominated:

What is one small change that would increase your integration score by 1 point?

EXERCISE C.2: YOUR FINANCIAL DUAL-CITIZENSHIP PROFILE

Two Republics, One Sovereign Self

Part A: Citizenship in the Digital Republic

What does it mean for you to be a "citizen," not just a consumer, of the digital financial world?

I am fluent in: ________________________________

____

I protect my digital sovereignty by: ________________________________

____

I contribute to online financial communities by: ________________________________

____

One digital citizenship behavior I will practice this month: ________________________________

____

____

Part B: Citizenship in the Republic of Inner Experience

What does it mean for you to be the "sovereign ruler" of your own psychological financial domain?

I know my financial triggers and wounds, and I respond to them with: ______________________________

____

I derive security from: ______________________________

____

I make financial decisions from a place of: ______________________________

____

One inner sovereignty practice I will strengthen this month: ______________________________

____

____

Part C: The Sovereign's Oath – A Personal Declaration

Write a brief oath that affirms your dual-citizenship and your commitment to integration.

"I, ______________________, do solemnly declare that I am a citizen of two republics.

In the Digital Republic, I will

____

____

In the Republic of Inner Experience, I will

____

____

I hold sovereignty over both. Neither will dominate the other.

I am the integrator. I am the author. I am the steward.

This I affirm on this day, _____________.

Signed: ____________________________"

EXERCISE C.3: THE CONTINUOUS PRACTICE AUDIT

Learning, Unlearning, Re-centering

Part A: Continuous Learning – Proactive Financial Re-education

Learning is not passive consumption; it is intentional study of underlying architectures.

In the past 12 months, I have learned about:

☐ How monetary policy or central banking works
☐ The incentive structure behind a platform or app I use
☐ Behavioral economics principles (e.g., loss aversion, mental accounting)
☐ The basics of a technology I didn't understand (e.g., blockchain, AI)
☐ The history of a financial event (e.g., 2008 crisis, tulip mania)
☐ A perspective on money from a culture/philosophy different from mine
☐ Other:

____

My next learning project (specific topic, resource, and deadline):

Part B: Continuous Unlearning – The Courage to Release

What financial "truths" have you held that may now be hypotheses to test?

Script / Assumption I Once Held	Evidence That It May Be Outdated	A New, More Adaptive Belief
Example: "I must own a house to be truly secure."	*Renting + investing may offer more flexibility and similar long-term wealth.*	*Security comes from my balance sheet, not the deed to a specific building.*

One outdated money script I am actively working to release: ______________________________

What makes this release difficult? ______________________________

What support or practice would help me let go? ____________________

Part C: Continuous Re-centering – Rituals of Return

Daily or weekly practices that bring you back to your core values and inner peace.

Re-centering rituals I already have:

☐ Morning meditation / prayer before checking finances
☐ Weekly financial review that includes values check-in
☐ Regular time in nature (unplugged)
☐ Gratitude journal focused on non-financial wealth
☐ Sabbath or digital rest day
☐ Physical exercise that clears mental clutter
☐ Other:

____

A new re-centering ritual I will begin this month:

Ritual name: ____________________

When / how often: ____________________

What I hope it will cultivate: ______________________________

After 30 days, reflect: Did this ritual help me re-center? How?

____

____

EXERCISE C.4: FINANCIAL MATURITY – YOUR VISION

Beyond Competence, Beyond Wealth

Part A: Defining Financial Maturity for Yourself

"Financial maturity is the capacity to move through the world of money with competence, clarity, and a deep, unshakeable sense of being at home within yourself, no matter what the future brings."

What does "competence" in money look like for you? ______________________________

____

What does "clarity" about money mean in your life? ______________________________

____

What would it feel like to be "at home within yourself" regarding money? ______________________________

____

____

On a scale of 1-10, how mature is your current financial self?

1 ☐ 2 ☐ 3 ☐ 4 ☐ 5 ☐ 6 ☐ 7 ☐ 8 ☐ 9 ☐ 10 ☐

What would take you to the next number? ______________________________

____

____

Part B: The Mature Steward – A Portrait

Imagine your financially mature self, five years from now. Describe a typical day.

Morning: ______________________________

Financial decisions: ______________________________

Relationship with technology: ______________________________

Response to market volatility or unexpected expenses: ______________________________

Evening reflection: ______________________________

What is one habit you can begin today that this future self already practices?

EXERCISE C.5: AUTHORING YOUR FINANCIAL NARRATIVE

You Are the Writer, Not the Character

Part A: The Story So Far – A One-Page Summary

Write a brief summary of your financial story to date. Include the key chapters: early imprints, victories, struggles, turning points, and where you are now.

Part B: The Genre of Your Story

Is your financial story currently a drama, a tragedy, a comedy, a quest, a redemption arc? What genre would you like it to be?

Current genre: ______________________________

Desired genre: ______________________________

What plot twist is needed? ______________________________

Part C: Letter to Your Future Author-Self

Write a letter to yourself 10 years from now. Tell them what you are learning, what you are releasing, and what you hope they have become.

Dear [Age]-year-old me,

With hope and intention,

Your [Current Age]-year-old author-self

BEHAVIORAL PRACTICE: 7-DAY INTEGRATION EXPERIMENT

Experiment Choice (choose one):

☐ **Experiment A: The Dual-Citizenship Log** – Each day, record one decision made from your Technologist mode and one from your Philosopher-Psychologist mode. Note how they integrated (or didn't).

☐ **Experiment B: The Ritual Installation** – Practice your chosen re-centering ritual daily for 7 days. Journal before and after.

☐ **Experiment C: The Unlearning Sprint** – Identify one outdated money script. Each day, write down one piece of evidence that contradicts it, and one new belief statement.

☐ **Experiment D: The Technology Fast with Reflection** – Choose one digital financial tool (app, notification, auto-payment) to abstain from or manually override for 7 days. Journal the experience of reclaiming agency.

Daily Log

Day	Experiment Activity	What I Noticed	Emotional State	Integration Insight
1				
2				
3				
4				
5				
6				
7				

End-of-Week Reflection

What was the most difficult moment of integration this week? ____

What was the most natural or joyful moment? ______________________

____

What did I learn about my capacity to be the author of my financial life? ______________________

____

One integration practice I will continue: ______________________

____

____

FAITH INTEGRATION

The Author of Authors

____

Scripture Meditation

"For I know the plans I have for you, declares the Lord, plans for peace and not for evil, to give you a future and a hope." (Jeremiah 29:11)

"Trust in the Lord with all your heart, and do not lean on your own understanding. In all your ways acknowledge him, and he will make straight your paths." (Proverbs 3:5-6)

"Look carefully then how you walk, not as unwise but as wise, making the best use of the time, because the days are evil." (Ephesians 5:15-16)

Part A: The Ultimate Author

If I am the author of my financial story, what is God's role in the narrative?

How does trusting in God's sovereignty coexist with taking full responsibility for my financial decisions?

What would it mean to write my financial story "unto the Lord" rather than unto myself or the world?

Part B: Stewardship as Co-Authorship

I am the steward; God is the owner. I am the author; God is the Author of authors.

How does this frame change the pressure I feel to "get it right"? ______________________________

What financial fear can I release today, trusting that the ultimate Author holds the whole story?

Part C: A Prayer of Integration and Commission

Write a prayer asking for the grace to live as an integrated, mature, faithful steward.

CONCLUSION ACTION PLAN

Your Path Forward

One commitment to my continuous learning:

One outdated script I will actively unlearn:

One re-centering ritual I will establish:

One way I will strengthen my Digital Citizenship:

One way I will strengthen my Inner Sovereignty:

One truth I will carry with me:

"The frontier of finance is no longer external. It is internal. The final, most decisive transaction always occurs between your ears."

CONCLUSION COMPLETION CHECKLIST

☐ I have completed the Two Modes Self-Assessment
☐ I have identified my integration gap
☐ I have written my Financial Dual-Citizenship Declaration
☐ I have audited my practices of learning, unlearning, and re-centering
☐ I have articulated my vision of financial maturity
☐ I have written a letter to my future self
☐ I have completed the 7-day behavioral experiment
☐ I have engaged with the faith integration reflection
☐ I have created my Conclusion Action Plan

Date Completed: ______________________________

My Key Insight from This Journey:

"Your financial life is, and will always be, a profound narrative. It is the story of your security and your daring, your generosity and your boundaries, your labors and your legacies. Technology provides ever more powerful pens and papers with which to write this story. Behavioral science offers a deeper understanding of the grammar and the hidden metaphors you employ. But the author—the conscious, value-driven, feeling author of your financial story—must always be you."

You are writing it. Today.

---

www.ingramcontent.com/pod-product-compliance
Lightning Source LLC
LaVergne TN
LVHW052216200926
848481LV00001B/119